Other books by
Stewart S. Warren

Shape of a Hill
The Weight of Dusk
Second Light

The Song of It

The Song of It

A Travelogue of Norteño
poems and personal stories

Dios te bendiga,

Stewart S. Warren

The Song of It: A Travelogue of Norteño, poems and personal stories
Copyright ©2009 by Stewart S. Warren

ISBN: 1-4392-4404-9
Library of Congress Control Number: 2009905455
Publisher: Mercury HeartLink

Book design by Mercury HeartLink
Portrait photograph by Jan West (www.janwestart.com)
Front Cover Photograph by Stewart S. Warren

Requests for permission to make copies of this work, or inquiries about public speaking or presentations may be sent to:

Mercury HeartLink
editor@heartlink.com

Additional copies
and other HeartLink
publications at:
www.heartlink.com

for the first people
for the newcomers
we are one and the same

Contents

I Know Why Gabriel Was Tired

Enter the Village with Your Hat in Your Hand

Silence, but That Was Just a Word

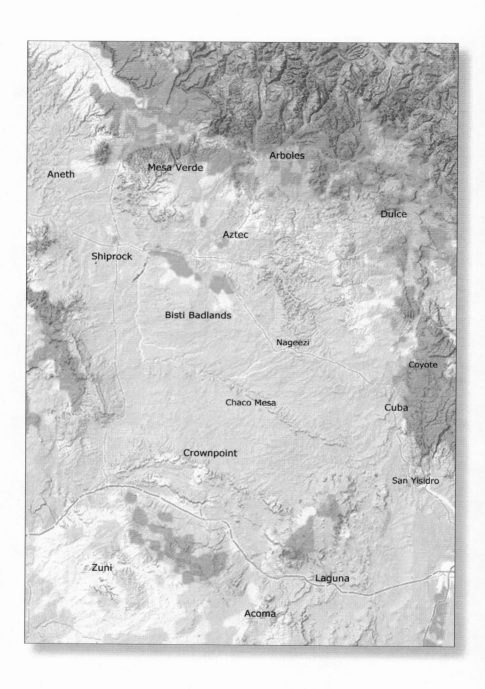

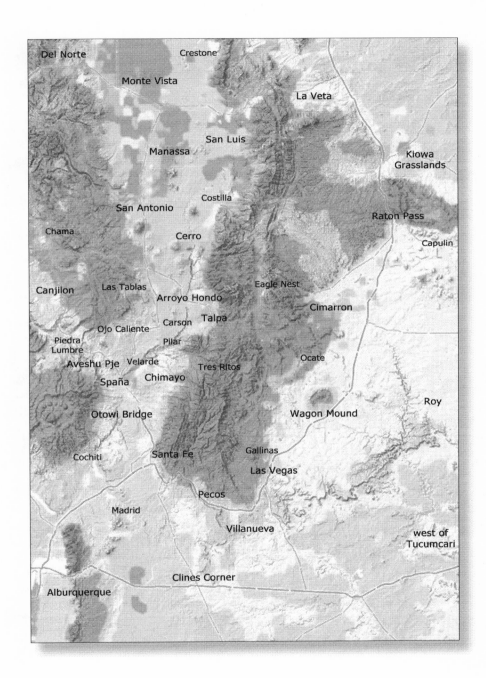

Good Way to Get Here

I begin in the East, the place of new beginnings. From there everything must follow its course. As an American youth all possibility lay to the West, the untamed, undefiled open road of chance—or so the story went. It was on that road that I sought experience, teachers and the opportunity along with others to scratch my own words on the back of the Needles, California city limits sign. It was on these roads that I found, and find, goodness in people and a genuine interest in one another's struggles and achievements, and more importantly, moments to join.

In preparation I made numerous efforts at hitting the road beginning with running away at eleven on a fifty mile jaunt through Eastern Oklahoma by coaster bike. At thirteen a friend and I stole some money and hopped a bus to Santa Monica. Not gauging our arrival with our age and California curfew laws, our glory was short-lived. Later that year I washed up on the shores of Galveston, Texas to work in the carnival until arrested (escaped and caught again) and returned to my hometown. School counselors were right to say I was escaping a hell at home, but that was only the part that helped to push me out. It's this fire within that I hope to address in my poetry.

A word here for Oklahoma: I will come back to tell those stories as well. It was there that I learned to take notice of "the lay of the land," fell forever in love with trees, and watched honesty and principle thwarted by poverty and discrimination shine even more clearly in the lives of people who were close to the land and close to one another. And though I admit it's sometimes more difficult for me to acknowledge the well-to-do for their sensibilities, it was from both my parents that I first learned to see beauty in the world: my mother weepy at a strain of music or arrangement of flowers, my father with his quiet appreciation of the land and his astute observations that stripped away pretense but left a deeper human dignity.

My father, who was born in Chelsea, Indian Territory (southeast of Tulsa), abandoned political life and the trappings of society after a wrenching divorce and became a recluse except for moments spent traveling the nearby country with me. We always had rifles and fishing gear in the trunk of the car, but mostly we looked at how rocks were formed or examined the etymology of words. He told me stories of oil-rich Indians buying new Cadillacs, driving them until out of gas, then purchasing another; explored a town that was soon to be underwater with the advent of a large dam project on the Arkansas River; pointed out Venus and Mars (love and war) riding either side of a crescent moon; and walked in silence as the tall winter grasses of the Osage Hills brushed up against us. He said, "I want you to see this country before it's all gone."

And so, at fifteen I began in earnest. After paying my respects at Woody Guthrie's house in Okemah, an abandoned homestead where poems had been scrawled in charcoal on the walls and a neighbor's goat on the hillside kept the weeds down, I got back on Route 66 and thumbed my way to the coast. I didn't leave Oklahoma for good, but once I rolled through that cap rock country near Tucumcari and felt the land lift me up like a giant wave, my sail open wide as the sky—well, there's never really been another. Though I have various places and people with whom I reconnect across the country, it is to Norteño (northern New Mexico) that I most often return, and where, in my home at

Nido del Cielo, I am now writing.

Some of the poems in this book have appeared in other publications but have never before been presented in a collection specifically Norteño. The prose, personal but brief, that accompanies these poems is new work and might be experienced as a running provenance. At times the two forms, poetry and prose, diverge with lives of their own, only to converge at other moments where they may illuminate one another.

You may approach this work in any way that pleases you: back-to-front, stuffed into your back pack, on the arm of your travel chair or read aloud to your lover. The sections have been loosely grouped by region, allowing the reader to settle into an area of northern New Mexico while exploring its culture, topography and essence. This is a travelogue of Norteño, but not of grand scenic overlooks, the best hostel in Santa Fe, nor the hidden location of sacred sites—you find all that stuff on your own. Rather, this book provides a catalyst for a shift in seeing. *What we see:* the beauty of a planet being formed in the moment and our good fortune to be intricately part of that, is often indescribable (though I try). *What remains* is just this: shared awareness and wonder without boundary or name—our true self.

Stewart S. Warren
Nido del Cielo, 2009

Who Has Called These Refugees?

Thunder Above

I found sanctuary
on the banks of the Rio Grande,
cut loose those skulls
I was dragging,
let the grass grow back.

I left you a trail
of cornmeal to follow,
but you already know
this undeniable sky,
the smell of good water.

The gate's open;
the colts in the corral
are tossing their heads.
Soon the mesa
will blaze with mustangs.

At Las Vegas, New Mexico

A goodbye is not immediately
a new beginning. Things take time
to count, not by numbers
but a value of horizon. The distance
to the next town depends
upon your wagon, a profusion
of mountain bluebirds, a day
or a year to let the wide sky
settle into your self.

Though you circle like a fox
at the base of El Provenir,
you may not find The Hermit.
Legends of saints run away
with themselves, lead back
to the fancy of their makers. But surely
the spirit of the pilgrim is with us.

Back at the Plaza Hotel the manager says,
these ranches will never be divided.
We're both believers, so by God,
somewhere it's true.
Somewhere the prairies run
without wire, somewhere
sunset pronghorns by thousands
take turns at the watering hole, the place
I always wait for you.

Near Gallinas a grandma lights candles

beneath the dry whispering cry
of a red tail, while brush goats grunt
and clatter along the ridge.
That grandma—she prays for me.
She says I have "the leg of the dog,"
always moving on, wild iris
running up hill with the wind.

I don't argue. Her prayers
are the water of my life.
She prays for you, too.

Adobe House

By the time we found it
the roof had already collapsed,
its gray vigas leaning
like telescopes against the wall,
melted mud sloping
up in the corners.

That which was house
was now being carried off
with silent water, invisible
waves of wind, with
the slow movements of sun.

The rain comes in.
The light comes in.
Small birds
fly in and out.

I find you everywhere:
on both sides of this dirt,
in the over-grown floor,
above the beam.
Make something of me
that won't last,
and when the last pink cloud
has finished
we'll go down sweet
in tall grass together.

Calumet Says

Of all the beautiful forms, grand and intricate, that the New Mexican landscape expresses there is one in which I always feel known and profoundly free, that of the grasslands of the Eastern Slope. As the mural of Calumet on the Grand Avenue Building in Las Vegas reports, this is the place "Where The Great Plains Meet The Mighty Rockies." Perhaps it's here at the entry to Norteño that the first two lessons are made so clear: You must let yourself be small in order to enter and, The land will choose what it wants to teach you... and when.

The Eastern Slope has that trick of perspective that lets you look out and think you're seeing it all in one sweeping eyeful—then something shifts: the light, the time of day, the wind, the cows, whatever, and it begins all over again. Because last time you looked you were on *that* hill a quarter mile west, and it was *that* time of year, and it was *that* sky, and *that* thought was in your head, and as vast and complex as it all is, it begins to come to you that the fact of your standing there and what's in your heart at the moment is having an effect on everything else. It's hard to form a solid thought around all this, and it's not something to share with just anyone, but never the less, there's a felt sense that it's right, and it's knowable, and it's bigger than anyone ever let on.

The Way to Ocate

If you're going to the fiesta
take the dirt road past Black Lake
where the eastern slope
opens to the grasslands,
to the golden rolling plains
and immediate sky;
where a wild stream falls
toward the heart of Ocate.

Hear that big guitar and Spanish fiddle
as soon as you top the pass,
see long tables set on the lawn
with bowls of posole,
platters of empanadas; children
spitting peach seeds
into the thirsty soil of Ocate.

Women with flushed faces
step from the porch
smelling sweet, their dresses
lapping like oceans
at the foot of a moon;
hollyhocks hold their breath against the wall,
the last amber light of dusk
washing over Ocate.

When flying finger clouds
turn the same shade of silhouette
as The Sangre de Cristos in the west

and the firelight makes a circle
of the whirling faces,
you can give yourself away dancing
beneath the shiny claws of night
pulsing above Ocate.

Sign Painter

Maxwell Turnip. That was the name of the white 1963 VW that I was driving when I left the coastal plains for the last time. It held all my worldly possessions, and the red primer bleeding through worn spots in the paint job gave Maxwell his vegetable namesake. It was the early '70s and "Trucking" by the Dead was the theme song. When I wasn't hitchhiking I was offering rides to other members of our amorphous tribe. This time I had a hiker with me from the East Coast who possessed an overall faith in the world but was indeed wide-eyed as we turned off on a shortcut through an Apache reservation east of Phoenix, Arizona. It was there that Maxwell coasted to a dead stop due to stripped splines on the rear drum of the drive wheel. We were, as they say, in the middle of nowhere—or almost. As we jacked up the car we heard drumming and singing just over the hill.

We walked up the hill, then crawled on our bellies the last few feet and looked over into a deep rugged canyon where at a distance we could see that a native ceremony was in progress. We couldn't determine if they were dancing for deer or preparing for war, but we knew we weren't invited, not to this one. Aided by the wind-kicked dust, the setting sun cast a bronze hue over the landscape, pinks and purples soon to follow. The strength of the drums and high pitched wail of human voices woke the mountains and made things that you thought were dead shine from the inside out. I left my companion to watch the car and witness this spectacle of the American West in the illumined silence of his own senses while I started walking toward the nearest town. The first car to come by gave me a ride. Soon I was sorting through parts in a salvage yard and found a brake drum made, not of South American steel, but of German steel, for this was the second time I'd ground that softer inferior metal to shavings while jamming gears through the mountains. I returned at sunset with the brake drum; we did some wrenching and were on the road again. San Diego for me.

Arriving on the mild coast of Southern California I stayed for a season. While working in El Cajon doing a carpentry job for a furniture store I struck up an acquaintance with William, an Algonquian who was somewhat out of place on the west coast and working at the car lot next door. When William wasn't washing one of the cars on the small lot or painting signs (for that was his trade) he hung around in the shack with the rest of the guys while they talked car salesman talk. The conversation was like an ongoing multi-narrated joke, "Did you hear about the guy who walked into the…," except the stories seemed to be about themselves, the car lot, a couple of local bars, and a few fantastic places in the world where you'd be hard pressed to verify any of their tales. To most of this William and I just listened. One day William confided in me that he was on parole. Having had a similar experience I never asked the reason. Details come forth as they're supposed to, at appropriate times and in appropriate company. You size people up in the moment and decide then and there if you're willing to go down the road with them. And that's exactly what William and I did, we hit the road after work one evening, doing the speed limit and keeping it cool until we reached the Arizona border.

William had his own Chevy that he had acquired through the car lot. (And again, I didn't ask.) It was a bright turquoise Impala and reminded me of a piece of sky through which a medicine bird was about emerge—swift and proud across the lower Sonoran

Desert. We traveled in tandem, stopping in roadhouses for drinks, but not staying long enough to call attention to ourselves or leave residue in anyone's mind. On the second night we pulled our vehicles over at a wide spot in the highway and parked under the only cottonwood tree within thirty miles—Maxwell, the turquoise medicine bird and a gazillion stars. The next morning I woke to find William gone, and except for one little coyote trick, all traces of him had vanished in the vast mirage of Arizona.

I had a toolbox under the lid of the VW with mechanics tools, stuff for wrenching on cars from a previous incarnation working at auto parts stores. Sometime during the middle of the night William had taken my toolbox and in its place left his toolbox which had sign painting tools: pencils, colors, tints, brushes, etcetera. That's the West I know: you go to sleep one night with an idea of who you are and wake up the next morning with a brand new occupation, a fresh start. Two days later I wrecked my car going up First Hill into Los Alamos, New Mexico and arrived in town as a door to door sign painter. A really bad sign painter. I was able to talk my way into three jobs before it was time to either leave town or change professions. My last sign was the entire glass front of the doughnut shop near the park that I painted during the middle of the night and that was unveiled the next morning by the rising sun itself to groggy coffee hounds. All of the letters had huge tails that gave the whole scene a feel of migrating pterodactyls drawn by an adolescent in detention center, and of course, it was done boldly in bright turquoise and pink—the colors of the Arizona desert in flight.

Frost

She's kissing everyone, dressing the dark world
    with a crystalline nap, coaxing water
        from the heart of everything that lives,
            "and," she says, "everything lives."

She's getting ready to wed the sun.
    Her silent breath forming tiny fingers
        at the edges of her gown, already
            reflecting the mind of her lover.

The bride-to-be stitches the last lace
    on tall grass, mud ruts, half-showing stones—
        on everything fearless enough to dream
            facing the deep black sky.

There Are Windmills, Lots of Windmills

Near Capulin last year's sand-colored grass
rides the undulating plains
on waves of the earth's naked crust
and two volcanoes sit north and south,
one a shield spilled in a flow,
the other a perfect cone.

If you rest your gaze windmills appear
one by one, then open clusters
across the pale blue curvature.
Silence by degrees reveals
Orioles twerting, whisper of bunch grass,
the crawling of lichen, hum

of distant ranges, their blue
tuned to oxygen, to your breath,
to the background ocean of beginnings.
Your body fits here,

a glove made of star stuff,
a looking glass on a hill, a wheel
that keeps saying *thank you*.
Sometimes you pretend to be alone,
an alien; you let one small pebble
do your thinking—give it to me;

I know what to do with it.
The whirring and knocking of the mills
brings up bucket after bucket;

that perpetual song of crickets
is you expanding...

Eagle Nest

Near the frozen lake a trampled swath
cuts across
the otherwise velvet snow—elk sign.
We too have arrived in great herds;
a memory of the earth
is a memory of our body.

From the foothills a single line of willows
marks the watercourse, sleeping naked, ready.
Today I'm renaming the peaks
above twelve thousand feet: Tara's Song,
World Peace, Cries for the Sun.

Each time I see you
I'm more in love than the time before.
It's cumulative: this breaking
and opening of the heart.
I hear the best fishing at Eagle Nest
is under the ice.

The Sport of Summer Rain

Through rippling torrents
the wet elms
pitch and hurl their heads
in warning.
Thunder and lightning
come ridding in
over the foothills.
A war party circles.

Green and purple flags are folded
into the tumbling charcoal sky.
Arrows strike my windows,
rattle the stove pipe.
The lights go out.

Suddenly the storm
wheels north, leaves water
gushing from my roof, peeling
the stones below.
Toward town I hear whoops
of warriors counting coup—
everybody running for their car.

Tall grass is tangled,
sprawled across the yard;
a tomahawk stuck in my door.
Sweet clover and thistle weep openly,
their hands drawn up
around trembling green hearts.

All is Well

When Cynthia had a visitation from her deceased mother just
west of Sipapu neither of us were surprised so much as we were
grateful. By then we had already entered the world of metaphys-
ics and had been experimenting with remote healing back in
Austin along with several other spiritual technologies. What
made this event special to me was the innocence with which it
happened. She simply sat down with a question in her heart and,
viola, her mother appeared and comforted her. Cynthia and I
had been given yet another gift and began to suspect, and then
to understand, that the natural world was not something to pry
open so that it divulge its secrets. Life, as it turns out, is more
than willing to be seen, ready and happy to be in relationship
with us at every level.

But the experience of contact goes beyond communications with
loved ones on the "other side." Along the way it occurred to
me that I could send a thought of encouragement to myself at a
younger age. At a moment of pure contentment and belonging
there arose in me a desire to share, to join, since at that moment
I *was* joined. I began calling across time (as if that was some
distance) to that boy who saw himself as alone and weak, "It
turns out okay," I would tell him, "keep coming forward." Later
I realized that the flicker of hope I had felt as a boy struggling to
be in the world had come largely from myself. It was my voice
of encouragement from the future, from now. This helps me to
understand whose voice it is I hear now saying, "keep coming, all
is well."

Alburquerque Flea Market

Mexican vendors outside the fence
pass cool *paletas* to flea market goers.
Overhead children squeal
for two full minutes
at the end of the Swinger;
then, the Space Shuttle.

Blue and white tarps stretch
in taut swells across acres
connecting havens of shade,
marking spots.
I move from side to side
in the flow of foot traffic,
in and out of pop tunes,
cowboy crooners, *musica especiales.*

I cross borders of incense,
pass through tents of boots,
after-market chrome,
custom covers, raw nuts,
air brush tattoos.
If you want socks,
see the Vietnamese. They know
about walking in the reign
of one intruder after another,
politics like monsoons.
Two for five, she replies,
when I hold up a bundle; and I wonder
if her sisters work the factory

where these garments are made,
how the poets of her childhood
sang of rice fields and frogs,
how she's come to know
the self she calls herself,
no matter what the market.

At the corner of sunglasses
and southwest art
I turn right down rows
of tools on tables, old movies
spread on blankets.
A Senegalese groove pulls me in
under faded batik.
Her man plays the log drum
while she comments
on the woven basket under my arm.
I set it down for her to feel.
We both know how round it is.

In ten hours this tent town
will tear down to a scattering
of smashed cups, corn husks,
the last truck swinging its lights
toward the gate; the global village
dispersing into the night—
a linger of tribal sweat.

On television they put us
all in houses. They expect
everyone to be watching,
to be lining up for product.

At the flea market we truck
tomatoes, hubcaps, handshakes.
We don't stay put
when they try to count us.

Staying Warm with Friends

That old Indian was laughing so hard I thought he'd fall out of
the car. We were driving around in circles on the reservation
dodging prairie dog mounds and steep arroyos in a fire engine
red VW Bug that I had acquired in a somewhat unscrupulous
manner in Los Alamos a few days prior. [If anyone knows what
I'm talking about I will gladly pay the $200 owed on that car.]

My new native friend that I met down on Central Avenue in
Alburquerque told me that if I could catch one of his cows I
could keep it. So I was sneaking up on them in the red VW, and
when I got close enough I'd jump out and start running at one
of the cows, arms out like I was going to hug a long lost brother.
There's just no end to the fun you can have with new friends,
cheap wine, and no sense in your head whatsoever.

A few years earlier, before my wrangling days on the Laguna
Reservation, I was coming through with New York Dave, travel-
ing in my '56 GMC. We made Santa Fe but the truck refused to
go any further. It was 10 degrees at mid day without a cloud in
the sky, and 22 below at night. A shop owner on Canyon Road
who made excellent Scottish Eggs took us in and also let us
use her stove to heat the crankcase oil in an attempt to get the
Gimmy started—to no avail.

That night we walked up to Claude's of Santa Fe, a bohemian bar,
with a fireplace wide enough to accept four-foot logs. A bunch
of Jemez Indians had come in off the res to stay alive (it was 42
below near Cuba, New Mexico) and so Claude's was staying open
all night as a kind of shelter during this reported coldest winter

in 62 years. The tribe had taken a half dozen tables and set them up to form one long table with the head "singer" at one end. He had the drum. We sang social songs like Pop Eyed Ford, songs that were okay to share outside of ceremony. After every round of songs it was customary to slam down a beer. As the new guy I simply followed protocol. Native Americans are said to have difficulty holding their liquor but from my vantage point under the table they looked like they had their shit pretty well together.

Next morning we abandoned the truck, hitch-hiked to Mexico by way of Louisiana and New York, and I picked up the Gimmy a few weeks later. After a while Claude's disappeared replace by boutiques selling imported alpaca serapes for a thousand bucks, but shelters of the human spirit continue to configure themselves at will and as needed—any moment an opportunity to join.

The Refugees

The refugees are coming, are coming;
they are coming from the cities and
when there is catastrophe in their streets
they come in waves.
Refugees from freeway shootings,
refugees from the plastic overlay,
refugees from the wounds of greed.
They come to escape, to remember, perhaps
because they have been called.

Who has called *these* refugees?

They visit in the fall
and move the next summer;
they think they've found paradise
but first find only a reflection
of their own billboard
made from movies, magazines,
Wild Kingdom on late night pot.
It was, after all, an idea of paradise
that they brought with them.

Who will teach *these* refugees?

The refugees get shuffled through
vague mazes of county inspectors,
indifferent clerks and a million mañanas.
So they apply more logic, more money, aplomb.
But a degree in Business or Anthropology

does not stop the neighbor's barking dog
who sometimes dresses up as the endless wind,
endless mud, miscommunication.

Who will console *these* refugees?

They come, and still they come.
These refugees are hungry in their
desire to touch this mountain;
they are angry in their futile attempts
to make adobe quit melting;
they are lonely in their
moments of world collapse;
and they are weary of waiting
for a God they do not know
how to trust.

Who will embrace *these* refugees?

At the Santuario de Chimayo

Two women approach the altar;
one crosses herself, looks up at Jesus;
the other steps boldly
to a statue of the Virgin
and presses a two-finger kiss
on the face of the Mother of God.
We find our own way
back to the river.
We find our way like those flakes of tears
and chips of dried blood that fall
from the chiseled *retablos*
lining the white plastered walls
at Chimayo.

The Santuario was built
on top of a healing spring—
just like my own temple.
Today I purchased another *milagro*
to bury in the earth, in the hole,
in the floor, of that sunken room
next to all those retired crutches
(how they hang like crosses
on the road to our waking).

I ducked into the narrow cell
and settled on my knees
below a cloak of candle smoke;
a chorus of red prayers flickering
in wrought iron racks—

proof that we can observe our own suffering.

I pushed my secret wish
into the cool damp sand and prayed.

I delight in the use of props: churches,
poems, lifetimes, planets and corn.
Everything has become an instrument!
Even my longing
feels like lightning
striking in both directions.
When we're remembering
together like this
I hear a river
with each of our names
tumbling toward the sun.

Voice of an Arrow

This is you
     gazing at the sun,
          bringing the world to completion.

Here is a hungry child
     crying on his blanket;
          you are bread in the wilderness.

Here is a bow
     bent against the night.
          Here is the way of a beautiful painted arrow;

it arcs endlessly
     across endless skies.
          This is the way: radiant, narrow.

Water, Life Blood

What can you take for granted?
The sea, that giant being holding
ten billion births at once;
this porous ground, fiery center,
infinite mind above;
the calculations of leaves,
when to turn, when to fall.

What can you name
that does not already
have an assignment?
This crooked bug on its way
to the queen, that red star
drifting on a breath,
the tendency of everything
to outgrow itself.

What wishes to be known,
sending intelligence
and healing from the future,
re-informing itself
as today's rain, today's blood,
this morning's saline tear?

Where is our water now?
The underground caches
of the Incas and Bedouin,
those dried lakes whose fish
we find pressed

sideways into mountains,
last spring's puddle in the drive.

What is the nature of her being?
Self-contained in any amount,
holding only a fraction of herself,
resilient, mindful,
a million places at once; a memory
that bends with the weight of light.

And tell me, how do you pray
knowing she is inside us,
riding her ribbons to the sun,
swaying in the rock of her cradle?
And how do you regard your neighbor
when you bring her to your lips?

Visit

On the banks of the Rio Pueblo
    just above Tres Ritos
        my wife asked for a sign
            from her mother.

In moments
    an iridescent humming bird
        appeared in front of her face,
            her spoon-shaped wings

rapidly scooping
    the thin mountain air.
        They looked at one another
            in the filtered light of morning,

in the absence of time, then
    her mother, as humming birds will do,
        left in a line
            diagonal to this world.

They Burned the Wrong Inipi

Buddy

We put Lynn's sewing machines in storage at Alburquerque and headed up the Turquoise Trail. I called them sewing machines. As a seamstress she had other names for them like Baby Blind Stitch, which was not meant to be an endearment but denoted the smaller version. I'm not sure if that's the one that sewed up-side-down or in-side-out, but she was a regular engineer when she sat down to do her work. We planned to pick up our stuff when we found a place to settle. The area we were passing through was not "Abbey Country," that would be Southeastern Utah. But it was where Edward Abbey and John Nichols plotted against the United States while driving down the highway shooting up road signs. Their blood alcohol levels are not discussed here.

Just outside of Golden, which could be anywhere 100 yards either side of the post office, Lynn's little Opal expired from the heat—a water pump issue. I assured her, while keeping one eye out for rattlers, that it would be alright and I stuck out my thumb. In no time we not only had a ride, but we had met three truly good people, a couple and their four year old son named Buddy. Buddy's dad was an outlaw and a biker and that would make Buddy's mom the ol' lady. They took us to their home in Madrid (pronounced with as much Texas disregard for the culture of others as you can muster) where we learned about the current population of this once booming silver and turquoise mining town. When the mining died the town lay nearly in ruins until, like hermit crabs, a migration of what society calls misfits moved in to occupy the one or two room shacks on the west side. A few unocupied and larger houses on the main street were vied for and the town was settled anew by outlaws, ex-cons, and otherwise alternative types. Very few paid rent. The law was raw decency and common sense.

Our hosts put us up for the night, fed us two meals, drove us to Santa Fe for a water pump, loaned us tools and helped with the repair—and never asked for, nor expected, one dime. Lynn and I dug into our pockets and flattened out a few bills which we gave to Buddy's mom. I took a snapshot of Buddy in the front yard, his little shorts sun-faded from spending his days outside in the blistering dirt, a plastic holster around his waist, a cowboy hat nearly to his eyebrows, and a cap pistol firmly in his right hand. If anybody's going to mess with his parents, his house and dog, or anyone else in the town of Madrid they're going to have to deal with Buddy.

At Madrid, New Mexico

Fool's Gold and shattered bottles sparkle between Cholla,
shot-up road signs, and at the bottom
of easy-to-lose-yourself-in canyons. Squatters
no longer live in the miner's shacks, but thank God
there's a few genuine outlaws left in town.

Some suit in Santa Fe put us, as they say, on the map.
Damn them! Damn their county court house grids
and get-away destinations. It's none of their business
what I keep under the seat of my truck.

I know a woman with a long skirt, a keen eye,
and more sweet milk than I may deserve.
And while I'm at it, damn those selfish bastards
who would exploit her in the name of liberation.
You think she doesn't know where water comes from?

Old-timers on the hill are tired; I don't blame them.
When the wind takes out a snag you can hear a sigh
follow that final crack. Enough is enough. Hell,
we've all been had, and nobody here can boast clean hands.

Every other corner's a dirt pimp, replicator of trinkets.
They tumble across the desert, so much momentary litter.
But don't waste your time on designers of distraction.
You've come from a good home; your heart is mighty.
You leave those dogs to me.

At the ball park they drive 'em low while Madrid's children

are learning to bridge the stars—creators returning the silver.
I'm sitting here talking with Mary at the bar in Cerrillos;
if it's a corn dance you want, go to Santo Domingo.

Fifty Something Woman on Canyon Road

It's a devilish curse: your shock
of white hair at the crown,
the length of your experience,
penstamen poise, eye explosion.
I'm a gonner

and we've just begun,
commenting on art
at the counter, what
our generation chose,
or didn't. I was shy back then.

This morning I want you
in that moment of rousing,
warm cupping, moaning
together. We'll take
half a day on the high road,

the other half coming home.
Every curve will be a slow turn;
mossy seep, altar to Mary,
breathless destruction.
Rising and falling

through afternoon showers, we'll break
into small town churches
and ring and ring and ring,
these scarlet mountains
melting around us.

Hotel Window

The maids arrive
and turn down my bed leaving chocolates.
The sky above the Jemez Mountains is fading pink
and other colors I can't possibly name.
Vendors on the street below bend
into stacks of Mexican blankets
and cover their silver with dark veils.

The streets of Santa Fe are full of lovers,
arm in arm they lean into one another.
Men and women, women and women;
what does it matter, the way we lean
into one another;
the way those Peruvian street musicians
steer the evening
into the on-coming stars?

In the morning—flocks of pigeons.
We create housing for them
in bank buildings and bridges,
make room for their healing presence
then forget we even need them.
They show up anyway; gathering
like rain clouds over thirsty gardens,
like those Tibetan monks that meditate
on the tracks at Auschwitz.

Behind us now
the new sun cracks

over the Sangre de Cristos
firing stacks of earthen walls;
adobe faces of riverbed brown,
shell pink, Abiquiu orange.

Down Water Street the Hotel St. Francis
colonial as pressed shirts, and beyond it
the cupola of Our Mother of Guadalupe,
her white cross slightly tilted
against dark Juniper. And,
as you would suspect: pigeons,
swirling in the updraft of our dreams,
knitting her belfry to the sky.

The Museum of Personal Passages

"This is grace,"
said my friend,
"setting fire to the thin
veil of your drama—
the *thin* veil," he underscored.

In Santa Fe there's a market:
La Puerta, it has nothing but doors.
Stacks of doors lean in rows
forming an ancient city
that turns and twists across
the hard packed earth.
Entryways made
by Moors, by Mexicans,
by the urgings of ownership;
ornate openings with spiral stiles,
faded red paint outlining
complex family patterns.

For a moment let's call it
The Museum of Personal Passages.
See the intricately layered gates,
deeply chiseled grief,
the grand access of Kings,
seductive statements of invitation,
delicate finger latches,
sunburst transoms, dark barricades,
elaborate frames.
Oh, how proud we are

of the body. How terrifying
the smell of smoke.

Today my door is smoldering,
hand rubbed lacquers blistering,
the core heating up.
It's too late to call
for the bucket brigade;
this door fashioned first by an orphan,
this old friend cut too short
across the bottom
where crickets sneak in,
these hinges that weep
when they sing.

"Sometimes," he said,
"grace knocks first—
sometimes not."

Salvaged

"June 6th," he said, "Invasion of France."
I found him slumped in a rusted 1930s lawn chair, the ones
when new you'd see facing the tennis courts of fine homes. This
afternoon he was at the end of a dirt path loosely defined by
used auto parts, junk appliances, and the otherwise discarded
extensions of our need for safety and convenience: a mound of
alternators, picnic coolers full of power steering pumps, jumbles
of rebar, some gnawed bones, a deflated beach ball. Mr. Lujan Sr.
was collapsed in the shade of Russian Olives growing along the
ditch that ran behind two house trailers, one of which was the
office of Lujan's Towing and Salvage in Española, New Mexico.

His grandson had winched my vehicle from the scene of a wreck
two days prior and now Mr. Lujan was explaining without
prompting the reason for his crippled condition: a spinal injury
incurred when his plane was shot down over French soil.
"Never even got 'em in my sights," he said.
Grabbing his homemade cane—a club with gnarled knob that
matched his hand with its deformed and shortened fingers—he
raised his body to a hunched, but never the less, standing posi-
tion. It seemed to take years, practiced and surrendered years.

As he hobbled into the bright sun I saw that he was tidy in the
way he dressed, his shirt tucked in, pants belted and absent of oil
smears. His waistline disappeared under a gaunt rib cage that
hung offset over what must have been his hips that day in 1942
when he enlisted for Uncle Sam. On our way to the gated aisles
of salvaged iron I told him of my accident, how the other party
never even slowed down as they roared through the light, spin-

ning me violently around in the Santa Fe Highway (clanking of
disembodied plastic and metal returning lifelessly to earth). As
the stubs of his fingers found the numbers on the combination
lock and threw off the chains I realized he'd heard all this before.
But it was my turn and he accommodated me with straight
forward compassion, a battlefield surgeon focused on service, not
on dramatics.

"Don't worry about the dog," he assured, "he's afraid of me,"
and taking the weight off his walking stick he shook it momen-
tarily toward a two-inch iron pipe driven into the ground around
which was a 12 foot circle of bare dirt. Nosed against the stake,
an Oldsmobile was the apparent shelter of Liberty, a Rottweiler
he told me, who at that moment must have been at the end of
the heavy chain disappearing behind a tire. On the other side,
and just at the edge of Liberty's circle of daytime patrol, was my
pickup.

I don't think of myself as one who overly identifies with
"things" or imbues objects with personality, but I admit a sink-
ing feeling at the sight of this crumpled mess that had been my
steed and part-time home for several years. Now it lay where it
had been lowered next to others, the life gone out of it—a wreck.

Cautiously at first, until I felt sure Liberty was at bay, I tugged
out arm loads of my recent life: seasonal clothing, binoculars,
tow strap, outlaw country CDs, a vial of sweet grass oil, and so
forth—the stuff we think of as personal and unique, but when
sorted in the middle of a salvage yard appears common and trite.
I thought to hurry, though it was unnecessary, while he leaned
patiently on his club surrounded by decades of injury and loss.

When I'd gathered the last load of work gloves and wool army blanket, I gave a final look at the impact, a truck trying to fold in half, an exposed rear axel absent of a wheel that was never found.

"Man," I exclaimed, a bit righteous, "she was really barreling through that intersection. Two feet forward and I might not be here talking to you."
"Pretty darn fast," he nodded, then pulling his torso up for eye contact, "but not as fast as the angels."

The Music of Norteño

Leroy's grandfather takes him fishing
at the lip of the Bazos, a hundred browns
to lug back to the truck.
Young bodies like E strings do the work,
los viejos are a slow walking bass.

These are tortillas back and forth
in her hands; these are eight cylinders
popping in the yard; this is the rhythm
of geese honking north,
a worried dog outside all night.

Ruben's hands torment the guitar,
his *rasguero* straight as a chair.
"*Baile,*" someone yells
from the back of the bar
and a redhead steps to the floor.

Furious violins climb and claw
at loose dirt, then the horns
single file down to the river.
A blind man tumbles out of the sky,
sweet sisters leaned against the rail.

Cool blue lights under the chassis,
a thousand watts in the trunk;
what goes down in the parking lot
is none of their *pinche* business—
the beat goes on.

In Truchas only a *brujo* plays
his flute after dark; see those girls
steal across the field. All of us
cross ourselves the next morning.
La 'cequia, el camino, la capia—
this, the music of Norteño.

Cruisin' con Los Viejos

Why my mother was driving a "muscle car" and the account of how I rescued her from the car—or the car from her— are stories for another time. Never the less, I drove that 1969 Pontiac *Custom S* with a V-8 engine the size of a washing machine and a Hurst floor shifter throughout the Intermountain West and up and down the coast for several years. I put gas in it and never looked at the bill. Donna and I called her Corn Flower.

When the time came I parked her in the front yard of my home in Talpa with a For Sale sign. That was the house with the ox blood floors, a term that refers specifically to the way the mud floors were sealed more than a hundred years ago. After all this time the floors still had a dark reddish cast from the blood and to accommodate the unevenness of the floor every piece of furniture had a shim under at least one of its legs. As is customary for older adobes in this part of the world, the wiring for electrical outlets was run on the outside of the plastered walls. That's Norteño: one afterthought after another, but a good ride parked out front makes any house fine. It always amazed me how Corn Flower looked so stylish and, at the same time so at home in Talpa, or anywhere else she was parked.

I had a couple of nibbles, as they say: a deputy, then some kids, but nothing serious. Then an older Hispanic couple from Española showed up, and in their quiet-to-themselves kind of way they checked out the car. Chipmunks touching a piece of the car, backing away, chattering to themselves. They said they'd be back next week to look at the car again. I told them I would leave the sign in the window and they understood. The next week they came with their number two son, the mechanic. He had all the right moves: popped the hood, looked at the end of the tail pipe, listened as he started, stopped and started the engine. The couple stayed in the yard while he took the Pontiac out on Highway 518, a demonstration of their respect for me. We talked about the longer growing season down in the valley, the rain, or lack of it, and so forth, while their son checked out the drive train and suspension. They spoke to me in English and smiled at each other when I said I got the car from my mom.

They were still interested, they said, and would come back the following week. This time I took the sign out of the back window. Sure enough, the couple showed up again, this time with their number one son, the one that went to school. For this session we met at the kitchen table while he went over the numbers, good registration, clear title, all that. I offered to cut the price in half and we were all happy. They gave me cash, drove back to Española and I went on with whatever I was up to at the time, probably setting up poetry readings and wild crafting medicine plants.

While washing dishes one day I heard a honk in the yard. Yes, of course, it was the sweet older couple from the valley, proud to the point of almost giggling. The *Custom S*, no longer Corn Flower, had undergone a few changes: some mechanical issues addressed, a new tucked and rolled upholstery, several coats of steel gray lacquer buffed to a gleam. They had all four windows down on the hardtop and were out for a Sunday cruise, radio tuned to Radio Lobo out of Los Alamos. I always thought that the '69 was the kind of car you'd pass on to one of your kids, but in this case it was passed on so this couple could be kids again.

Riding with His Brother
for Patrick

Low and slow at first,
a faint throb and rumble
of distant thunder
like a lonesome blue dream
on the single dirt lane
called Camino de Simón:
in the baking sun—sand;
when it rains—a slippery stream.

In La Puebla all are christened:
the ditch, the sheep, the Monte Carlo
creeping into view, wide mouth
of the front grill about to speak.
Chrome reverse wheels
with spokes and bullets; Mary
reflected in every surface.
No hydraulics, just dropped.

Pulse of longing, this
is a *memoria* to a brother
snatched from his motorcycle—
a mystery wreck.
In Cholo script on tinted back glass:
In Loving Memory of Isaac.
Cruisin' slow classic lines roll by,
slope of pearl finish falling
across the trunk.

Española with a Pack of Matches

I'm careening through your narrow
sandy streets, beige
and pale pink in dusty sun;
I'm keen on the cut of your cars,
low and slow;
I'm wounded by your family style
of voting and keeping score;
I'm thinking in a hotel,
in a room where Jesus stayed
between fishing trips,
the courthouse and the grave.

Everything here is hanging
by a thread: blood red ristras,
fly paper, sponge dice,
the fate of a foreigner.

These high ceilings could be Egypt,
a place he once called home,
afternoons with astrologers and mathematicians,
crocodiles on the floor, cats at the gate,
his father waiting on another dream.

I'm standing in a single room
studying this pack of matches,
wondering if I should torch this thorny town,
set another village on fire.

Sometimes I walk backwards,

throw hand grenades and mirrors,
but every cause I've fought
has been for justice.
But every battle has hurt someone.

Compassion is a blue ghost
vanishing on the river,
disappearing down another alley.
I think she may be living
in Alcalde or Chamita.
I'm headed there tomorrow.

The Writing Class

Patty passed around copies of poems,
her handwritten assignments. I swear
I could see the pressure of her pencil
on the words "unfair," and "torture."

Her brothers drank and fought
at the kitchen table, shooting
at anything that moved; stopping only
to regroup for another verbal attack

on some Anglo *pendejo,*
the family taking sides.
Patty lived in Spanish, labored in English
to find a voice strong enough

to put an end to it,
big enough to nurse them all.
I wanted to give her more words,
a machine gun with verbs,

windows, ventilation in her kitchen.
I wanted to dynamite that table,
burn it with description,
push it away with alliteration,

but every week she brought us back
to that fist rattling the dishes.
Her pages like the splattered wall
behind her stove were decorated only

with the grease of blame and crucifixion
where she pressed her ten line poems
into *tortillas,* thin as torn flesh,
ladling up the meat of the matter.

That Indian's Back

Ten miles up where yellow cottonwoods
close above the Rio Fernando
patches of trout beside bent golden grass
hold the township of Shady Brook.
Susan waits tables on rough pine
with a two-way radio on her hip,
someway to call the cook
who's across the road fishing. She says
she knows something about that Indian.

The Golden Indian wasn't always gold.
He came over from Oklahoma
or Arkansas wood naked
with a Thunderbird on his breast.
She painted him gold
a hundred years ago, that second owner
when she bought this place.

His right arm raised a shinny hello
to the first automobiles in New Mexico.
Gas pumps with glass heads,
bottled beer, brisket, folks up from town.
Nobody knows how many times
that Indian disappeared.
Lassoed by school boys then drug
up and down the road
is a trail of dirty tears, bad luck
if you keep that nickel,
the Indian always came back.

Thrown off a truck after three years drunk,
or maybe he spent a lifetime
with a Tewa girl, brought deer
and honor home to her family.
Where would you go
if you were painted and tired of standing?
The last owner dressed him
in a top hat and skeleton mask
for Halloween photographs.
Imagine kidnapping that.

Susan brings a decaf with desert,
says, I'll tell you something else,
there's ghosts up here,
I've seen 'em moving
across the veranda at night.
Sounds like that Indian's got relatives
up from Pahuska or Little Rock.
Why else would he come back?

Last time he showed up
they brought him in off the road,
stood him in a garden next to the kitchen
cemented in the center
of a small oriental pond.
Seven Chinese Koi
now flash gold at his feet.
They swim with fourteen brown trout—
the cook's idea.

Nothing a Volcano Can't Handle
(but get down on your knees)

New Mexico I see your walls
crumbling, hear bulldozers growling,
their heavy chains dragging,
tearing off sheets of skin.
Juniper bodies piled high
in mass graves—cremation
without even a prayer.

Hold on New Mexico.
Stone-face them, lie to them,
set their god damned wagons on fire.
Everybody wants to feel you up,
the tops of your breasts sun-blessed,
exposed. Your poverty
now an easy target,
no longer something sacred
belonging to the ground.

Your feet are still kicking, pushing
toward El Paso del Norte,
but already the casinos have eaten
their way up your heart line;
glittering legal malignancies
to dress you up
then take you down.
It's time for purification, New Mexico.
Pray for volcanoes.

Intelligence

Unusual Animal Death—that's the new vernacular. Up until the evening that Phaedra called I'd known them as cattle mutilations. My friend Phaedra arrived in the '60s on the Hippie Bus as a part of the caravan of Merry Pranksters led by Ken Kesey that crossed the country experimenting with consciousness and community aided by psychotropic substances. One afternoon she and I visited the old bus at the location of the Hog Farm Commune near Llano where it rested peacefully in an overgrowth of native sunflowers. I took a picture of her standing in the door next to the hand-painted inscription: "Nothing Lasts." We talked about karma and choices in our lives, about roads taken and not taken and her history in Taos Valley. Phaedra lives in Upper Hondo within a stone's throw of the original Morning Star Commune where for many years she has raised children, animals, vegetables and consciousness. A journalist and photographer, Phaedra, like her father before her, is also in the newspaper business. She had recently been investigating UADs in New Mexico for The Taos News when she was contacted by a rancher about unusual circumstances in her own neighborhood. It was about this new and unexplained incident that she called me.

She brought me up to speed on her work, the Unusual Animal Deaths that she had investigated around the state and the findings of others in the field. She then filled me in on this new situation in the Hondo Valley, explaining how a cow had been found by its owner who was disturbed by the evidence of its death. A long-time Hispanic rancher in the area, he was convinced that the cow he found in his pasture had not fallen at the jaws of usual predators or anything else with which he was familiar. Phaedra, who saw the cow before it was buried, said it had all the markings of a UAD. Uncanny stuff. What was even more concerting to her was how the rancher abruptly changed his story after being *interviewed* by government officials. After that he dismissed the whole thing as being a coyote attack. The next day, at Phaedra's request, we went to Hondo to help her with closure, perhaps some understanding—at the least a friend who wouldn't blow her off.

We parked our trucks on the highway above Herb's Lounge and walked east into the field. The cow carcass had been moved to higher ground near the 'céquia, and then buried with a back hoe. We sat on a blanket near the grave and said very little to one another. Phaedra had brought her guitar and sang a song or two. I had brought the sacred pipe which we shared simply and with little religious protocol. Nothing psychedelic about Kinnikinnick or the inner bark of Red Willow—prayers transcend all that. We then fell silent, and with closed eyes we journeyed on our own for a spell.

Soon after getting quiet I was visited by a white faced cow, one of the clearest visions of this type that I've ever had, and an exceptionally strong presence. Starring gently into my being, this representative of the Cow Clan transmitted a powerful message to me, the essence of which referred to a contract between humans and bovines. At that moment I understood that cows willingly entered into a relationship of service to the human beings. It was an act of volition, of love. Nothing docile, submissive or lopsided about this relationship. It made me think that perhaps there are other contracts as well with other species, and I hope we're keeping up our end of the deal.

Phaedra and I may not have gotten the kind of answers for which we were initially looking, but when we stood to leave a feeling of increased peace had moved into us. Without talking about it we both began walking back by way of the 'céquia under the cottonwoods, though it was clearly the longer route back to our vehicles. In a few moments we came to a stand of juniper and a small clearing within it, and there, another cow. I would have walked right by it, passing only a few feet away, if Phaedra had not stopped me. How could I have missed it?

We examined the body and found that it had been disemboweled, all the inner organs removed along with the ears and some flesh on the skull. All of this had occurred without the slightest ripping of skin; nothing ragged, random or hurried. As if with a laser scalpel, very selective parts had been taken, leaving the bone clean and white. There were no signs of struggle. There was no bloating. There was no blood or other fluids present. There were no flies or gnats near the body. There was no smell. And even more significant for me, there was no trace of energy whatsoever, emotional, psychic or otherwise. Nothing. It was hard to guess at causes when we were still puzzling to accept the effects.

Some people regard Unusual Animal Deaths as myth, others as yet unexplained scientific phenomenon, and still others speculate that, like crop circles, they are the manifestation of our collective thought forms. I don't know. But I was reflecting on a response that Ken Kesey had to a question about his use of psychedelics, about any concerns that he might have damaged himself. Ken said, "You don't get anything free; everything bruises something—so you trade off." That's somehow part of Karma: interrelatedness, cause and effect, a seemingly endless number of opportunities to get the lesson, the surety that we will.

A couple of weeks later Phaedra introduced me to the work of Dr. Stephen Greer at a conference in Colorado. Stephen was heading up the Disclosure Project. He had obtained and was assembling the testimony of hundreds of high ranking and notable individuals from the scientific and military communities including astronauts and admirals. All of them were reporting evidence of encounters with extra terrestrial intelligence of the 1st and even 2nd kind. Stephen's goal, like that of Dennis Kucinich with the Department of Peace, is to effect a shift in consciousness at the level of government.

The possibility of life, far more intelligent life at that, existing beyond (and within) our world is threatening for some people. And for those who thrive on systems that are derisive, any information that might unify our species is unacceptable. What if, for example, we were shown, and were able to utilize, an energy source that would make hydrocarbon fuels immediately obsolete? The particulars of things like UADs, psychic contacts and wrecked space ships will morph and present themselves as necessary. What seems much more important to me is opening to the intelligence within all species, terrestrial and extra terrestrial, including our own.

To Cochiti, Across the Mountain

Tyuonyi [kee-OH-nee], "Meeting Place," was a principal city
of the people now called Cochiti. It was inhabited for
an estimated 400 years ending in the mid-1500s.

Beyond the plateau of birds
and above the grid
where streets are named
for madmen and bombs, the clouds
billow in natural wonder,
grasshoppers snap in sunlight, and trees
rock rhythmically in meditation.
If East is thinking, West is feeling;
if South is doing, North being.
I have friends in all directions,
a task at every turn.

Aspens lean and creak
into one another at the edge
of open spaces where Harebells nod
toward undetermined futures.
If I lay down in this high meadow
I could nap and dream, or
I could wake up
with the earth for a face,
a smiling mind.

Oregano de la Sierra, strawberries,
Paleo, Queen Anne's Lace; how could we
talk ourselves into starving?

What grows from rock breathes with it,
sends tiny stars shooting on the wind.
My hand rests lightly on lichen;
I, too, older than granite.

Before I could see, I was given visions—
a generous gift for a man
so blind and stubborn.
I thought they came from another world.
In some ways I was right.
The angels I send return.

Over mountain marsh: murmur of thunder.
Standing on a blade of rock
above lower peaks
(soft green in morning mist)
I tip my wings
toward *Tyuonyi*, a place once
of doing, now, being.

Return to Taos Village

We all have our own icons, preferences
for red or green chile,
star-clinking nights alone on the mesa.

I came back for a habit of moon;
for the smell of red hot rocks
as sweet grass is brushed across their faces.
I came back for the baby.

In the village I visit from house to house. The brown earth
of streets is the same as the hard brown earth of walls,
hornos, hands, courage.
Each of us is a mud room sharing common walls;
I frame this mountain through every doorway.

I spread my blanket on the floor
and light candles for the dead—and for the living.
I'm a traveler welcome in the kitchen,
another loaf of bread added to the circle,
a trail across the sky become visible.

All the Red Chile

All the red chile in Velarde
and miles of ripe melons
couldn't hold you any longer
on these dusty and rutted roads

and miles of ripe melons
and thousands of honey, I'm sorrys
on these dusty and rutted roads
with poverty naked in the ditches

and thousands of honey, I'm sorrys
and you trying to make me see
with poverty naked in the ditches
that this was never your place

and trying to make me see
holding disdain as your shield
that this was never your place
this clanky silver and bitter sage

holding disdain as your shield
in front of that frightened child
this clanky silver and bitter sage
this landscape harsh between us

in front of that frightened child
with frost bitten fingers
this landscape harsh between us
never hearing the apples fall

with frost bitten fingers
you went back East
never hearing the apples fall
for all the blood of our effort

you went back East
couldn't hold you any longer
for all the blood of our effort
all the red chile in Velarde.

Burn This Religion

Eventually all the water let loose upon the land that does not evaporate finds its way to the Rio Grande. This is how it is in Taos Valley. There are four primary drainages that traverse the valley, one by one connecting with one another before falling inevitably into Taos Gorge: The Rio Lucero, Rio Pueblo, Rio Don Fernando de Taos and the Rio Chiquito. In the southwest corner of the valley they all converge into what remains the Rio Pueblo which then begins cutting a deeper and deeper canyon until it becomes one with the Rio Grande at a placed called Taos Junction. A one-lane dirt track cut into the side of the canyon hugs its contour all the way down to one of the few bridges across the Rio Grande, and then back up the other side through Carson and eventually to Ojo Caliente. Before the avalanche I took this road once a week to visit with my teacher, Thomas One Wolf.

Thomas, whose mother was Suquamish, was passed as a young man to a teacher from Diné who, also from mixed blood, taught him the ways of the Ojibwa. So Thomas was not a stranger to sharing across borders and working with many paths, and beyond them, to experience truth. I appreciated the breadth of his knowledge, his generosity, and the relaxed nature of our relationship. I had previously been involved with a group of non-natives (mostly Anglos) who were connected to Lakota elders up on the plains, and in our scramble to get it right, which never seemed to happen, we were rigid to a fault, often missing the essence of spiritual practice. So when I met Thomas I had a lot of energy around doing it right. I wanted to be a worthy student, to learn the correct ways of native spiritualism, to receive an identity, and finally to heal the disconnected fragments of what, at that time, I thought was my self.

Thomas wanted to do it right, too. But mostly he enjoyed the pound of bacon and carton of Marlboros that I brought every Friday. And he enjoyed sitting around the one room cabin smoking, telling stories, singing songs and passing the day without unnecessary cares. Like many "medicine singers" who make themselves available as teachers he acquired somewhat of a following and that following became a community, and communities become messy. Teachers are always under the gun. They become somebody's mommy, somebody's daddy, someone to take the rap for humanity. No path is without ego, and anything involved with ego is disappointing. I, too, became disenchanted for a spell before coming through the lesson. But before moving on to new teachers and teachings I facilitated ceremony with him on one of his trips to Trabuco Canyon at the base of the Santa Ana Mountains.

On the next of these adventures with his students in Southern California the ceremony of four simultaneous sweat lodges was halted when a Lakota traditionalist showed up with her armed goons to protest the appropriation of her spiritual heritage. People were ousted from the lodges as Carol Standing Deer's assistants began dismantling the inipis (sweat lodges), insisting that they be burned. Thomas asked that his students not resist, but help them take the lodges apart, and together they fed all four inipis to the fire. Later Thomas was asked why he helped them and why he wasn't mad. "They burned the wrong inipi," he said, tapping his chest at the heart. "Inipi is in here."

The Low Road to Taos

Pilar, you are a good hello,
an awkward goodbye.
I was an eagle there
coming and going; never
the same river, always
the same thirst.

What moves in me has been
assigned its own fire, a peak
above the sky, an endless ocean.
I stretch heaven
into days across the prairie,
then, this church of canyon:
Alcalde, Velarde, Embudo;
soft black, hard rose, whisper
of hawk, torrent of moon.

Pilar, your bed is a smashed guitar,
a mud floor where travellers left
paintings stacked against the wall,
corn meal, sugar, coffee, smoke
from clearing the fields.
You are the entry
to three worlds, a pillar, not of salt,
but when I look back
my body disappears.

Outlaws Finish their Business

He slipped away from the crowd as the priest was finishing up at the grave and it occurred to me, given the circumstances and who was there, that he could be going to his truck for a gun. A couple of heads nodded slightly giving a clue that something was about to go down, something important, and I didn't know if I should leave or stay. The world of Taos Valley doesn't stop for funerals, they're an intricate component of daily life. In fact, the day-to-day busy work thought of elsewhere as living is the distraction here. Births, weddings, funerals—that's the medium around which all else is organized. And no matter how much money one has or doesn't have, everyone has a black shirt for these special days. Today Wal-Mart clerks, woodcutters, government workers, bereaved cousins, cholos and vatos had gathered around the grave in Talpa to toss handfuls of dirt on the box that held the body of Sammy Maestas.

The night before I had gone to the rosary at Our Lady of Guadalupe, sat in the dimly lit sanctuary while hushed voices mumbled the beads, whispered condolences and considered revenge. Intermittent gasps of grief escaped like vapors from the molten earth of sorrow. The casket was open for viewing and in spite of the randomness of activity there was a respectful staging with no apparent orchestration that kept the procession passing by the coffin limited to just a few at a time. Someone coughed toward the back of the church, a kneeling board hit the floor, a candle finished in a wrought iron rack giving off a wisp of pungent smoke and a side door opened and closed with a creak.

At the front of the church Sammy lay nestled among urns of

flowers, his body filled with fluids and dressed for deliverance. The hole in his forehead was puttied over, a faint crease added to show thoughtful expression, the face colored to suggest that he was not entirely gone. Bull shit—Sammy was gone. His girl-friend had shot him point-blank between the eyes when he tried to intervene and break up an argument between friends over a drug deal. Perhaps there's more to it than that, always is. When there's loss in a family we're good at drawing lines, making up stories, laying blame. Murder in Taos Valley drags a chain across everyone's door. It wasn't finished.

The month before the shooting Sammy had come up to the treatment center where his mother, Maria, and I both worked. He said he'd turned a corner on his life and was cleaning up. He hoped to help his friends get straight, too. He didn't want treat-ment, he just wanted to be in a safe place, make a little money. I understood. He worked for a week or so cleaning out flower beds. Maria worked as usual cleaning rooms. I worked cleaning up baggage-laden addicts where I'd quote a line from Hans Solo in the movie Star Wars, "We have to jettison the garbage before we can hit hyperspace." But as I was finding out very few are really interested in that kind of travel, not with all the family gravity and history of the world pressing upon us.

"It's done," the priest solemnly nodded to Maria, and with his layered skirts and sashes swaying about him, he strode passed the life-sized statue of Jesus frozen in time and dragging his own cross through the churchyard. Then the padre disappeared behind the windowless morada and we were left to our own understanding. With everything done according to the church it was time to get on with the unfinished business at hand, the business for which most were waiting. After removing himself from the circle, Sammy's cousin grabbed something from behind the seat of his truck and returned to the grave. He shouldered a guitar and began strumming, then softly singing, the outlaw's anthem: Bob Dylan's *Knockin' on Heaven's Door*. Most people kept their gaze toward the hole in the ground, occasionally looking up into one another's eyes and throwing an arm around a waist or leaning into a shoulder. Handfuls of dirt echoed brightly on the box then grew more muffled with each toss.

"Moma, come take these guns from me. I can't shoot them anymore." Swaying and sobbing we sang the chorus for Sammy and we sang the chorus for ourselves. "Knock, knock, knockin', I feel I'm knockin' on heaven's door." Then, it was done.

Wood Pigs

Wood pigs! That's what Rob called us. Beginning in late summer we'd cut and haul our own fuel wood. Pigs? It has to do with those mando mounds of split wood beside the house. No tidy New England style stacks for us. There are some very practical reasons for tossing the wood in those seemingly haphazard piles, but that's secondary at the moment. Size matters and you might as well let the world know it, and if your wood pile reaches the eve of the house... Hey.

One year we went up Rio Grande del Rancho. It was Halloween. Our first snow always seems to fall on Halloween and that year it was right on time. Toward the end of the day we were working a steep north-facing slope, selecting the Douglas Fir—more BTUs, easier to split. We'd fall them and buck them where they fell, rolling the blocks down a ravine toward the truck. The light was turning and the snow was getting heavier. It was one of those moments when you look up and realize everything's getting away from you—in a hurry.

Rob yelled, "I'm gonna do this one more guy right here."
I scrambled out of the way of what I thought would be the trajectory of this two ton grandfather tearing through the canopy. Rob made his cuts, yelled something definitive, and... nothing happened. Shit.

Maybe he hadn't put enough angle on his cuts, maybe the wind was working against him. Whatever. Rob crept up to it keeping his stance in the slippery snow and tried working his saw into the back cut, but the tree kept rocking, pinching the bar, stalling the chain.

"Shit man, what are we going to do?"

"Nothing *to* do but get our butts out of the woods while we can still see our way down the mountain, that's what."

The woods are like that: one minute you're king of the mountain, the next minute you're very small and having to deal with your ideas about that. We talked a little about that tree at first, then it moved to the back of our minds where it rocked and creaked up in the mountains all year long.

Next year we headed into the woods a little early and the first place we went was back up Rio Grande del Rancho. It was still there—amazingly—cut in half and waiting. It was Rob's business to finish it, and he did. An excellent job. We figured that was good medicine as the rest of the year went well as far as wood cutting was concerned. Later on, however, Rob and I had a falling out. I decided one day to give him a piece of my mind on a couple of accounts. That is almost never a good idea, not for me anyway. I cut too deep, and though I made efforts, there was just no repair. Wood pig, that's me—but there's still a tree up in the woods that just won't fall.

Lord of the Children

The Lord Of The Children
looks down on his village
and sees blue windows
opening into old mud,
sees giant cottonwoods
in late afternoon,
their trunks deeply grooved
by years of crying
into the forgiving earth.
Inside the village: frybread,
plum jelly, some horses, clowns
on the opposite roof.

Beyond the stables he sees
two pickups parked in a field
exchanging secrets for dope;
sees the dirt road turning
to asphalt, cyber arcades,
police dogs, plastic force.
At sunset he stands
with eagle fan and remembers
his many nieces and nephews.
He sees the turning of their lives
like the naked trout that twist
in the stream that runs
through his village from east to west.

At sunset he climbs down
through four stories of quiet eyes,

speaking to no one, gathering
Grandmother Blessings,
following the well-worn wooden rungs
to make his final descent
into the circular earth.

As he passes I nod: pray for me, Uncle.
Then the Lord Of The Children
washes his hands in curling smoke
and takes his place around the drum,
sending frybread, mountain water,
and fresh horses
from the Center Of The World
to the children who are far,
far from home.

Falling for You Again
a song for Taos Valley

I look for you in late afternoon
leaned against adobe, street boom,
bougainvilleas on the veranda,
hips and drinks clinking
in the hotel lobby.

I browse for you in the super store,
double CDs of Dylan on sale,
a snap-out sun shade,
patchouli turning my head
toward faded jeans.

I search for you in the back streets
of Ranchos' dusty single lanes,
squeezing through rock walls,
Choke Cherry, Paleo, persistent sage.

I look for you in El Prado
cruising with the Goddess,
Super Sport low and slow, Trans Am,
Surround Sound,
Impala ready for chrome.

I wait for you in Talpa
at the stock tank, shuffling in dust,
sculpted salt lick,
drone of dizzy flies,
kinda shy, kickin' shit.

I watch for you at water's edge
on Rito de la Olla,
long legs and swooping wings,
powder gray, muted blue,
timid eyes, off again.

I listen for you in the peep and tweet
in tall grass, the rustle of piñon
and salt cedar, singing mountains,
power lines, screen door bang.

I look for you in the layered haze,
horizon's endless game and flaming plains,
Tres Orejas, Cerro Azul, Miranda Canyon,
the dying sky with its fading rules.

I dream of your gypsy traffic
and blinking light,
your hollyhock walls and acéquia madre,
your orchard basket view,
blue trim, red sky, honking enthusiasm.

I stretch my arms to hold you once again,
your enchanted blood
and runaway slaves, your passport
that is always red, your heart
the same color as mine.

Swimmer

On Easter morning we gathered in our back yard for a community send-off under huge Live Oak Trees dripping with Wisteria that were blooming forty feet high into the mild Hill Country air of Central Texas. Friends had arrived at daybreak to set up tables with quiche, sweet pastries and other yummy delights. This was Cynthia's one request for going away presents; mine was live acoustic music. Everything was ready. Our friend Paul, who in later years became Paula, was our scout, the driver of the U-Haul and good companion. Dakota, Cynthia's Border Collie pup, would ride with she and I in the Blazer. It had all been planned and provisioned. Cynthia gave a month's notice at the psychiatric hospital; I closed out a private counseling practice, and we both packed and cleaned while I read my subscription to The Taos News. Easter, resurrection, new beginnings—we were on the road again after eleven years in the nurturing cocoon of Austin.

The following morning, April Fools Day, we woke to blowing snow and colder temperatures as sunlight was being torn to sheets that raced across the Eastern Slope—springtime in the Rockies. Arriving in Taos, we stayed with Wally and Glenda for a couple of days while searching for a place to rent. In those days the pickings were slim to none. It was a two month house-sit for an over controlling owner in Dallas, a horse stall in Seco or a moldy adobe in Arroyo Hondo. We chose the adobe and were soon (sort of) settled in a block behind Tito's Central Market.

Tito, along with his dogs, ran the one room *tiendita* with boxes and cans of products that you thought only existed on kitchy

1940s posters. If you needed baking soda, Quaker Oats or Mrs. Stewart's Bluing, and could catch him at the store, you were in luck. It was also a good place to hang out, drink a soda, and hear the news that didn't go into print. But throw away your high school Spanish textbook—this is Norteño, with dialects and *dichos* preserved from the Conquistadors and idioms added, but not recorded, by a people who remain isolated mostly by choice. For me, it was all an adventure: getting eyebrows singed off while lighting the oven, avoiding dust devils that can throw you up against a car, finding pot shards in the side yard, and caballeros with blood-stained chaps clopping up and down our dirt road at any hour, day or night. But not so for Cynthia.

I had returned to northern New Mexico sober and married, a bit of formal education and a trade, a house full of stuff, and a vision (or waking dream) in which I had been told specifically why I was incarnate as an Anglo. My earlier years spent on the road had left me with the knowing that deliverance may be the next kind soul to come along, new riches of experience and community wait around every corner, and, after all, nothing lasts. Circumstances are for learning and enjoyment. A *tourist* drags his place of origin with him, judging everything and everyone by it. A *traveller* appreciates nuances of culture, differences in perspectives, and knows that even this magnificent and beautiful planet is but a stop along the way. Besides, I hadn't grown up with poverty. The kitchen walls stained with pork grease and the crumbling adobe houses of the village couldn't harm me.

"Sweetheart, think of it as a foreign country," I said. Cynthia, on the other hand, grew up in the impoverished Italian sector of a small town in Ohio where most people worked at the Ford plant (if employed at all) and drank, boasted and grumbled in corner taverns while she and her little sister dodged bill collectors by hiding under the bed. She was absolutely freaked out by the bare light bulbs and often toothless *viejos* of Arroyo Hondo, a life to which she had vowed never return. And I, cavalier and boyish husband, provider and protector, could not save her from sinking below the swell of her childhood fears. By September the marriage had gone completely overboard.

While we were surviving one another's increasing emotional withdrawal, spring thaw had swelled the Rio Grande to a torrent of rock-cutting run off. One day Wally and Glenda invited Cynthia and me on a rafting trip through Taos Gorge. We were going to "shoot the box." The Taos Box is a stretch of river six hundred feet below the rim between the Hondo and Junction Bridges. There are no other take outs between these points—once you put in, you're in for the duration. Our boatman was a gentle giant named Peter Hanson who was well experienced with the gorge, meaning that he not only had the ability of a poet when it came to reading the river but a tremendous respect for it as well. On the trip with us was Denise, Peter's wife, who, after months of counseling with him, was in his company to see if their was any possibility of continuing with their marriage. It was all so tenuous: the precarious existence of these New Mexican villages, our relationships with one another, a run on the Rio Grande at the beginning of the season while most rafters were waiting one more week for safer waters.

There was so much that Peter (and Denise, for she had been on the river scores of times with him) had left out of our orientation, the things that if we'd known we might never have come. But we got the basics, the necessary and confidence building stuff: "high side right, high side left, brace, paddles up, etc." Peter gave an extra tug on the cinches of our PFDs, told us where to find the throw bag in case we had a "swimmer," and, most of all, to pay attention. As we passed under the Taos Gorge Bridge on Highway 64 I imagined the onlookers above us saying, "Look, honey, a boat," and taking pictures of our tiny yellow dot of humanity passing six hundred feet below them, suppressing the urge to throw something, anything, off the bridge. That was our last connection with civilization. Up ahead: Power Line, and if I had paid closer attention I might have seen Peter's jaw tighten ever so slightly as we neared our first serious rapid.

It's difficult to guess the weather above the rim and beyond the narrow slit of sky. A storm of any kind can roll without event across the valley above you, or swoop suddenly down like a wraith and breathe a cold hell hollering through the canyon. A team member pulled on another layer as our sunny day in early June grew darker and purple swallows dove from their mud houses into the cooling electric air. Many years before, builders had used dynamite on the rim above when running power lines across Taos Valley. A jumble of basalt boulders had been released and tumbled into the river below creating a 13 foot drop in the river's elevation and an opportunity for our initial baptism in the Rio Grande. "Power Line coming up!" Peter, standing just rear of center with his mammoth paws gripping the oars, called for paddles up and then braced and stroked and twisted and pulled, bringing us through our first boat-eater without carnage. We were in—for better or for worse.

The beginning of The Rock Garden, a long series of drops, pillows, holes and wave trains, was where we lost Denise. Sitting toward the rear of the boat, she had been popped out in an unsuspected moment and was now nowhere to be seen. And aside from risking everyone else's life, there was nothing that Peter could do except continue to navigate through this long and treacherous stretch of class III and IV rapids. "Swimmer." The term hardly describes the reality of being caught and forced through this almost endless torrent, the power of the earth reshaping itself at will. "There she is," someone yelled, but too far away to be helped before she was sucked under again. I flashed on the spillway at the end of the gorge above Velarde where the water is backed up in a small reservoir. A friend had told me that's where Search and Rescue looks for lost boaters on the third day. It's called the Body Trap. I looked at Peter's face; he was looking at the river. He knew (as his wife knew) you only get a couple of chances to surface in this kind of water. It's the fatigue, the lack of oxygen, the likelihood of cracking your head, of being held under in an endlessly flushing toilet.

Then Denise was there again toward the rear of the raft. In a moment of instinct Wally grabbed her life jacket and rolled back into the boat with her. At the end of The Rock Garden Peter maneuvered into an eddy where we disembarked onto a sandy shoal and assisted Denise into wool clothing, checked the severity of her hypothermia and examined her bruised leg. Cynthia and I were chosen to hold her between us in the front of the boat for the rest of the run. Denise's intermittent shaking and lack of color were disturbing, but there was something else in her eyes, something she wasn't telling us—the worst rapid was yet to come.

Just above the Junction Bridge, and at a place where spectators take pictures of capsized river runners, is a rapid that can toss boats end-over-end. It's called Sunset. With the bridge and the pull-out beyond it now within sight there was one last wag of the dragon's tail, then we could say we had "shot the box." Peter poised himself with a slight bend at the knees, Denise snuggled in between us, and for one last time Cynthia and I were truly a couple in service to others. Peter guided us safely through Sunset in a moment of brilliance, but if anyone took our picture I couldn't say. If they had, the image would have been of all of us holding one another against the storm but looking exhaustedly in different directions.

After our day on the river Peter and Denise, though they loved one another dearly, decided that there was no more future for them as a couple. A month later Cynthia moved in with Wally and Glenda before heading back to the familiarity and comfort of Austin, Texas. My relations with Cynthia's supporters were strained when they tried to control her visits with me during those awkward months of disengagement. They seemed bent on the good guy/bad guy game, and whether they had a genuine interest in Cynthia's happiness and as well as mine, it no longer matters. Cynthia and I are running our own river, and when it's all said and done the picture of us shooting Sunset will be of two bright souls laughing their bodies off.

We Face the Mud Together

On the high end of Dead Dog Road
under those three cottonwoods
the road makes another sharp ninety
down through the Cordillera: water snakes,
cattails, Redwing Blackbirds.

The high water table
generously informs the tingling roots,
flows silky mud across the road.
I don't have any children of my own.

But there is a place inside me
where I could kill another man
to protect this moist palm of wetlands
    though I know
my first choice must always be
to invite a man to see himself
in the shiny mud;

to make it safe enough for him
to fall on his knees and whimper
like the tender white roots
of the Chicory and Milkweed.

I Know Why Gabriel Was Tired

The Angels of Autumn

In this season of sweet grief
the vultures gather
in great towers,
circling above the desert,
calling the names of their kin;
a bird tribe assembling,
a double helix spiraling
between earth and heaven.

All summer these dark angels
have been cleaning up
the dead flesh of unusable forms,
of drowned mice
and discarded words,
of fallen sparrows
and murdered dreams,
the road kill of our desires,
the slough of our living.

Then one day they are gone
and we wake
to the sound of their leaving wings
scooping toward Senora and Torreon.
And in the silent
thunderous crack
of this autumn sky,
in the emptiness of it all,
someone is finally resting.

Morning Walk

The landfill east of Costilla
pushes dead appliances
and gut-spilled garbage bags
up against the foothills, and bird shit
streaks the rusted iron bins
full of human excess, excrement, mistakes.
At the edge of the failed and discarded,
resplendent mountains push back.

The solid white expanses
of The Culebra Range are hemmed
with dark forest of juniper and piñon.
Raven and Junco fly here, and,
as I said, Magpie.

Across the border snowy peaks
shimmer blue with a psychotropic patina;
a few lenticular clouds hover in formation.
This is the place
where The Suffering and The Rapture
are indistinguishable. My heart
can hardly hold the magnificence,
the authority of it all.
On our way to Amalia: Magpies,
so completely black,
so completely white.

Wide Track

Last week I put a 'for sale' sign on the old 69.
I've knocked out a lot of poetry
in the front seat of that car,
surfed 101 above the breakers,
followed storms to their blue-green conclusions.
On the Eastern Slope,
where Calumet tips her hat, I've sat
invisible with all four windows down
watching antelope sail across my lap.
Makes you wonder
just how many worlds there are.

Sheriff's deputy dropped by,
wants to buy it.
It's a muscle car alright,
that Hurst shifter is stock.
He says he's got to ask the boss,
you know, the wife. We both chuckle;
that's the way cars get sold.

There's a dirt short cut from Taos to Chama
if you don't mind the five extra hours.
That Pontiac's name is CornFlower.
I've done it twice now, back behind
San Antonio Peak, oil pan for a skid plate.
Sheepherders and vaqueros
got summer work up there,
think this big blue car is a curiosity,
twist a smoke, touch their brims,

take the reins and settle in.
We wait twenty minutes
for those little doggies to get along.

Bristle Cone Pines lay all blown down,
bone gray in a lightning field
where Cruces Peak is watch tower
from Santa Fe Baldy to the Sand Dunes.
At 10,000 feet chrome is ethereal
and Cornflower's an endangered species.
But that deputy, he's an asphalt man,
so this part's just between us.

Spider Lodge

North of the Guadalupe Mountains and down in a shallow canyon that runs to an abrupt wall which drops another four hundred feet into the Rio Grande Gorge is Spider Lodge. Last time I went there the sun bleached ribs of the inipi that we had constructed were still held together with frayed jute, and the grass growing through and around it made it look like a skeleton on its way home. I remember it at an earlier time covered with blankets, bright flags flying in all four directions, and the unique metallic smell of lava rocks cooking in the fire pit, a ceremony in progress.

We called this area Two Blankets, as Raven Hawk and myself were both on vision quest at different spots just a few yards below the rim of the gorge, she on one side of the smaller canyon, me on the other. Without consciously knowing it I had faced myself west with a wall of black basalt (congealed lava) behind me. For four days there was not a cloud in the sky, but I knew better than to pray for changes in weather. On the second morning, a Sunday, I was sitting on my blanket, 404 prayer ties around the perimeter, feathers tied in the rocks overhead, that suspended-in-time-feeling of fasting and the mammoth shadow of the east rim draining down the opposite wall of the gorge. Then it appeared as sight and sound and force: a fighter jet just below the lip of the gorge at eye level.

An Air Force pilot, probably from Colorado Spring, was taking a $10,000 spin around the neighbor that morning, staying just below the lip of the gorge to avoid detection. It's strictly against regulations to fly military jets in Wild and Scenic Rivers but at Mach 2 there's nobody that can pull you over and give you a ticket. The dark gray beast was suddenly there, and then not there, with only enough time for me to look up and see the silhouette of the pilot's helmet in the cockpit about 30 yards from where I sat on my vision quest blanket. The roar was beyond auditory, so when I use the words "shock" and "wave" I mean them as technical terms in the science of physics.

My outrage at this military display of excess and power, as immense as it was, seemed miniscule in the face of it all, and it occurred to me that day that I was going to have to make room for this—and this, and even this. Because if that pilot was having the time of his or her life sporting about on a summer morning, I needed to also be experiencing the fullness of my life according to my own proprieties. And perhaps I didn't know as much as I thought I knew about the design of the universe and who gets to play here, and why.

One thing I did begin to understand more deeply as a result of that was the connectedness of things. That morning I experienced every being, the animate and the so called inanimate: trees, dust, birds, rocks, bugs, the air itself, hold its breath, withdraw, and then slowly open again like shrimp eggs laying dormant in the desert for a hundred years until there is sufficient rain to support life again. I had thought that a transcendent experience like that would come as I sat crossed legged in a mindful state that I produced through prayer with sage and copal smoke wafting from a shell in front of me; perhaps a spirit bird delivering a feather. But there it was again—I don't get to choose the curriculum, only whether or not I show up for class.

94

Mogote Peak Sleeps

> "If humanity wishes to save itself from biospheric
> destruction it must return to living in natural time."
> —Pacal Votan, circa 680 A.D.

Everybody wants to know
where we came from:
Azteca, Barcelona,
Mandinka, County Clare.
In every language
we're called "the people."
Did my family have dishes,
carved things, customs
connecting us to light
and its movements?

—these unanswered cries
circling the summit of Mogote.

We arrived blue eyed
from Iberia, black skinned
from the coast of the mother
(sometimes secret in our prayers);
taking heads for the queen,
hearing the crack
of a colonial whip.
Have we had enough of chains?

In a rush on gold
or other high-ended icons,

in a frenzy to claim a stake,
to push through skin, we arrived raw,
toughened up on iron ore,
dirt farming, much blood.
Was our cause noble then?

—these unanswered cries
circling the summit of Mogote.

We brought bellies
of brown babies up
from other mountains
still smoldering above
civic temple grounds;
hauled pianos, dance steps,
clocks through the swamp.
Did we save things of value,
preserve the best of our kind?

San Antonio Mountain
had it's day, blistered to the top,
a bubble of magma,
a finger on the trigger
of earth's inner core.
But that wooded hill above the Conejos
we call Mogote exploded,
an orgasm of flying fire.
Will she clean this plate again?

—these unanswered cries
circling the summit of Mogote.

Sorting Pintos

Beans the shape of sleeping babies
scuttle through your fingers,
ticking into the pot
on the corner table at Rosalinda's,
grandmother and granddaughter
hands checking for small pebbles.
Rocking your beans.

These are your fingers, grandma,
brown and creased,
a little stiff this afternoon.
These are your fingers, *mi hita*,
slender shoots unrolling
in the sunlight of family tradition.

These are your fingers
turning the page,
letting the inedible *piedritas*
fall the other way.
This is the day
you decided to the let
the skin of the world wrinkle
and release like a wave.

At the Rio Grande County Museum

We pieced the town together
from faded archives:
daguerreotypes and old photos
taken at about the same spot
at the end of Pine Street.
We determined the year
by the trees planted there.

At first there were none
in this sand and pickaxe town,
just the buildings they would adorn:
the livery stable across the road,
the house next to mine—
tenuous and exposed lives,
but nevertheless determined.

Then the cottonwoods came,
natives that grew fast,
knew where the water was,
then fell apart, easy to burn.
After that, spruce trees, real mountain folk,
were plotted north to south, giants
that list leeward, fat as barrels;
three still standing at the church.

A party of flowering crab apples
danced up one street, down another,
leaving calling cards at the homes of the elite,
a flutter of petals on the first few dates;

at the end of the season, something on your boots.
Then, like rabbit ears on top of the TV,
a trend of push-over poplars came and went.

Last year the town planted sunburst locust.
They put one in front of my house;
in the fall it's the first to turn.
But no matter who we invite
to live among us, they, like ourselves,
grow weary of straining toward the stars
and come to suspect there's another way home.

The Hope of Rain

I could tell you about the rain,
about things that aren't here,
about things that dream to be
but have no parents nor soil
in which to grow.
The hope of wood
is to be burned,
the hope of lilacs to return,
the hope of soldiers
is still unknown.
Perhaps the hope of rain
is to mix with your tears.

Every town should have an angel.
The angel in our town
was named Gabriel.
He pulled a child's wagon,
shuffling discarded items
up one street, down another,
timeless but not eternal,
his wings singed beyond flying,
crumpling tin cans like you would
wash the hands of children.

I could tell you about the rain
in Del Norte because
today it is not here
and cannot defend itself.
We gauge the moisture

in our fields by storms
gathering on the mountain,
a song that takes two days
to reach thirsty ears.
The names of those new towns
planted as subdivisions
in wetlands and wild canyons
bare the names of beings
(elk, bear, horse, whooping crane)
whose pictures can still
be seen on the Internet.
I know why Gabriel was tired.

I could tell you about the rain
if I could remember
the freedom with which it fell,
the way it loves corn,
the mud where you once
planted your feet, the smile
across the valley when the sky
opens at the other end.

No doubt, someone will try
to steal you, make you
believe in shopping carts,
in religions either for or against—
anything to take your land—
and if you believe that
it belongs to you, then
it can be taken.

I could tell you about the rain,

about how it always knows
its way down the mountain,
how it will always find
the face of Gabriel.

Nodding Toward Antonito
for Aaron & Michele

A big valley heart, he said,
and I nodded inside
as if I knew what that meant;
as if the cranes had risen
a mile above the valley
(as is their custom)
and we both looked up
at their high haunting chortle
at the same moment
in familiar wonder;
as if the same hoar frost
had grown and crept in the night
with fuzzy frozen hands,
one crawling
along grandfather branches
of the ancient manzanos
of Antonito, the other
waving a wand of crystal
over the pueblito de Del Norte
causing everything
to catch its breath;
as if my new brother
had said the word tortilla
and we both thought mother.

But today started
with the deafening fog
pulled up close

around the autumn ears
of honey locust and cottonwood
and when it began
to burn away I stepped
onto my porch to visit
with my neighbor Larry
who is brown
and has a black dog,
and I am white
and live alone
with a cast iron skillet
that is always oiled
and flowers when I can,
and the Columbines
along our common fence
are buttery yellow
and nod this way
and then that,
and if you look up
there is nothing between us
but the big sky of the valle.

Larry is going to Alamosa
for a hair cut this morning
because, he says,
if it gets any longer
he'll have to get a dog permit.
Buddhists prayer flags
flap above my head
and we both admit
that this little town
has had the shit

kicked out of it
and makes us crazy,
but today, the 23rd of September,
it's God dammed paradise

and I'm thinking that my brother
and his wife Michele
must also have buttery Columbines
growing in their town.

Bad Weather Dicho
for James Tipton

"Cuando viene la lluvia muy fuerte
en la noche, recuerda tu esposa
con un beso."

"When torrent rains come
in the middle of the night,
wake your wife with a kiss."

Though all the petals are torn
from the roses, jackals run loose
in the capitol, venomous thoughts
strike at the mind
and sharp-edged tongues
howl like dry axles for tallow,
what better can we do?

In the roar of raging storms,
the cry of breadless mouths,
the cross hairs of blame;
    in this moment
when your lover's breath
is the only house worth entering,

turn into her hair, her cheek,
her thighs like loafs, your hunger
coming in off the road.
Wake your wife with a kiss

and swim and swim and swim
together to the shore
of exhausted salvation.

Journey to Thanksgiving

Across the Colorado border we are still
in the San Luis Valley, all our senses
stretched to inescapable surrender.
We say it's the floor of the valley
because that's where we walk,
distant snowy ranges
fading jagged into pale blue.
I say it's a wide bowl, a watering hole
reflecting the sky in each hoof print,
in every small dune drifting.
We are working our way through buffalo,
working through unconscious flailing,
through the memory of repeatedly
cutting off our own hands.
We are on our way to Crestone Needle.

Miles from any mile marker
the signature of a single tree
leans east, looks back
squinting into the long wind.
You could be tough as nails here
and still be pulled from this assignment.
Across the valley cottonwoods flow
from dark mountain wombs
and onto the golden grassy flats.
Twisting watercourses guide
red willows into focus,
their shinny stalks bobbing
with the lifted weight of magpies.

And near the town of Crestone
one horse hollers to another
in that urgent velvet way
that horses sometimes do
when stamping alone at a fence.

Inside we make a fire of hands
around sweet potato and cranberry.
We are souls interpreting resurrection,
homemade biscuits rising in the oven.
What are we waiting for?
I can't think of one injustice worth claiming
in lieu
of what's being remembered.

Tipping Wings at Dusk

The two great gate keepers along the southern entry into the San Luis Valley are San Antonio Mountain west of the Rio Grande and Ute Peak to the east. To me they're old friends marking the way and witnessing my passage along the routes taken by entrepreneurs, trappers, scoundrels, traveling priests, Indian slaves, Mexican *pobladores* taking possession of land, Utes and Apaches chasing or being chased, De Vargas, Pike, and the dubious Kit Carson. The list goes on, and my name is on it.

I'm just as likely to get off on a dirt road as I am to travel the two primary highways, winding my way through places like Jaroso, Mesita and Lasauses. Not many people know what's out there, what's spooking around in the San Pedro Mountains and the hidden wetlands, and those that do know are not building web sites to get you there. But I'll tell you this much: if you take 8th Avenue east out of Antonito you'll end up on that one lane wooden bridge across the Rio Grande with a little different look at the valley.

Late one afternoon in the middle of winter we left the road for a more elevated view. My friend Chris Knox invited Donna and I to fly up the valley. We left Taos Airport about an hour before sunset in a somewhat frail three-seater that reminded me of a barrel with a chain saw fixed to the front. North of Cerro de la Olla we flew over a large herd of elk, the same herd of over a thousand that spends several months of the year on San Antonio Mountain. They were spread out over a mile or so of snowy plateau. When they heard our plane they began moving toward center, coming in from all directions to a point chosen by them but not understood by us. We made a wide circle to have another look while Chris kept the craft at a respectful distance. Their trails across the snow were spokes of an ancient wheel turning with the momentum of survival. I would not have missed this spectacle for anything; and I also wished in some way that we had never seen it, never added our footprint of observation.

Several minutes later we skirted Mount Blanca with its expanses of pristine snow, pink in the majick of twilight, rising steeply from the floor of the valley then thrusting into the upper atmosphere. The sand dunes below us were mottled in their own ripples of deepening shadow, remaining illusory at every elevation. The grandeur of this land makes it appear so permanent, stable, formidable, and yet, once we have observed it, it is changed forever, and hopefully so are we—but how?

It seems that Manifest Destiny with its dominion over the earth and over unsuspecting others has pointed us toward extinction rather, as it purports it will do, toward insured survival. And while I describe some of the things I see, there are places I have no desire to paint, to write, to take back into my world. There are moments when I want only to sit together on a wild grassy knoll with our individual thoughts, our proximity and our shared breath. No need to investigate, to make a thing reveal itself. And I think there will come a time when we choose to leave entire planets teaming with life untouched, satisfied only, and completely, with knowledge that they exist.

This Perfect Place

The seasons move on without waiting,
stroking the mountain sides
in transverse veins of shimmering gold
or satin snow
and opening the healing sky
another blue mile or two higher.
Across the valley new piles
of potato rock are dumped
along scruffy fence rows
and in the un-irrigated corners
of fields, those patch-work triangles,
four to a quarter, that become
a hog pen or a hay stack,
or the resting place of retired tractors.

This morning those mounds
of million year old river rock
are the color of the peaks
above timberline—which is to say,
a thousand base coats of light
beneath an infinite spectral array
of hay, barley, buckskin and mallard wings
beaming back to space;
and along with it
an occasional yellow ribbon
faded white, its welcome
washed out by last season's sun—
and the season before that.

I don't know any soldiers
who have come home yet,

but this wide majestic
and mysterious plain flooded
with quiet and prosperity
between The San Juans
and The Sangre de Cristos,
(between Christ and his disciple John)
seems to me to be
a perfect place to work.

A perfect place
to raise buffalo and cattle;
a perfect place to grow potatoes and grains
for hungry human beings;
a perfect place for woodworkers
and wire pullers and store clerks
to notice the grace that runs
along the edge of every transaction;
a perfect place for artists
to lift up uncompromised beauty;
a perfect place to raise children
and to read to them
and tell them stories
of hope and integrity;

a perfect place where we can work
undisturbed, diligently,
on the things that have momentarily
slipped the minds of those
who are quarrelling elsewhere.

Nudging the Fire

I lit the fire at sunset,
  a bright nest of flames
    whipping in the wind,
      pink bellied clouds

giving back their flush
  of borrowed color,
    the usual dogs of Del Norte
      raising hell, releasing the day.

With a long wooden staff
  at the edge of the fire
    I nudged the branches
      toward consumption,

toward the maker of days
  and gave it all back
    to the tide of darkening sky,
      sand tumbling toward a wave.

*Enter the Village with Your Hat
in Your Hand*

Return to Posi-Ouinge
known to some as Ojo Caliente

Forget everything you know
and everything you think you know;
enter the village
with your hat in your hand.
These walls, the ones still standing
and the ones slipping into river,
they know the ways
of coming and going,
and soon so will you.

All summer long
those split-tailed swallows
swoop in and out
of their mud houses
under the veranda,
maintaining the great lodge,
connecting sky to land,
the faithful to water.

Everyday at dusk
Angelo lights the fire
as the other fire keepers do
along the Rito Caliente
and the Tsama.
Watch as he places
each ocher piece of piñon just so
and the sweet smoke,
taking another day to heaven,

makes you feel that maybe
it would be okay
to stay another lifetime.

Up on top: mustangs.
In the morning you find
the soft turned-up earth
of their dancing and know
that what they do
is none of your business.
They kicked off their shoes
generations ago
and in the secret fury
of their night our world
ceases to exist,
if indeed it ever really does.

But you don't have to go
up on the mesa
to watch the ancients
make points and bread.
You are standing
in the center of time
and everything you touch
will take you home.
You are the village now.

Las Tablas

Petroglyphs whisper back and forth along the cliffs, the old river road slows through somebody's front yard, winding between the main house, the capía and the horse shed. Under cottonwoods a scattering of dusty leaves on bare earth, orchard basket, tricycle. There are no casinos on this side of the river. The gamble is a fall wedding, one more run for leña in the old green pick-up, a court appearance in December. Sometimes it's hard to find this mesa.

I pivot around chile and corn, follow the Tusas River valley thinning into wild: Ojo Caliente, Madera, Servilleta Plaza, Petaca, Las Tablas. You can see the movement of satellite dishes, broken bottles. Someday we'll explain to our children how the video stores came after the churches, how there used to be moments where silence was the color of long fields laying fallow. Maybe Cipriano will come back to plant these fields when he's finished with that school. In the mean time I will pretend that I do not hear the crawling of golf courses.

Comanche Ridge rises steep, golden pink in that last hour of sun. For twenty miles now a cap rock outcropping of orange knuckles has held the valley in line like the bold stitching on Grandmother's cloth. I look for her in the tall yellow grass that tufts around propane tanks and drowsy cars. Once you get to Las Tablas there are only two ways out of the narrowing canyon. You approach the turn like a road crew coming upon a wounded dear at dawn. You want everything to matter.

By dusk the dirt road has become a path curving between boulders, rising through small stands of aspen glowing like poltergeists. Follow the trickling waters until they disappear. Break through the timber. Pull yourself up on the table. You are standing in the plate of the world; the last luminous blood of the Sangre de Cristos draining into the sky.

Listen...

a coyote.

Ojo Night

Snow settles on the heads of cooks,
dishwashers and security officers;
collects on their common boots
as they joke with one another.
Snow sprinkles the laborer's hands
as he turns the water pipe,
comes to the call of the shopkeeper,
splits the rest of the wood.

Snow gathers on the shoulders
of desk clerks as they make
their rounds, chat with a guest.
Snow swirls into the laundry
as a blessing on the workers
who fold sheets in pairs;
their chatter, their constant touch.

Snow drifts against telephones
where administrators work late
on numbers, the paperwork
that also makes it go.
Snow flurries on the faces
of maids rushing to prepare
the last room in the inn—just in case.

Snow whispers outside the room
where pilgrims are wrapped
as miracles in muslin and wool,
and it blows along the river

where a dog barks at her tail,
looks back at the village
in snow, all quiet, all warm.

Snow bathes the Cerro Colorado,
its gift of hot water from rock,
where the village rests gently
beneath a star brighter than most
that appears to anyone now
hopeful enough to look up.

Snow mixes with incense of piñon
and a prayer settles sweetly
on those who are still here
and those who have moved on.
And once again, and by its own forgiving,
the village is connected and safe
under the blessing of newly fallen snow.

Manuelito Rises Above the Spa

Manuelito floats his bronze box
up and down this rib of road.
Ojo Caliente, Shadow Mountain, Gavilan.
His office is the parking lot

of the only grocery in town. Truckers
break hard; tourists honk in paragraphs;
locals say, *Ah Viejo, get out of the way.*
They say he used to drink, a veteran

bumming money in front of Oliver's
and down at the market in Spaña.
Is it a crime to go slow? No, but, oh,
how the new abhor the old.

Manuelito shits himself again; no one
will take him in. His car has become
his wife, his casket, a faithful sailing ship.
Float, Manuelito, float

through small towns that hang
between cell towers where children
text like pigeons, and the moon
is neglected but determined for our love.

Manuelito pulls into the resort hotel,
a dozen ravens escort him over the bridge—
a time zone confrontation, an area code collision.
Women in strings complain he stares at them,

at the bodies they believe to be themselves.
But the war pulled his own body out
through the sockets of his eyes,
now, his eyes just stare. Float,

Manuelito, above the bell hops
and thousand dollar beds, the underside
of your machine tipping angel wings;
just enough gas to clear the trees.

Going On with the Wind

My friend Joe is a retired law man living in Ojo Sur with his wife and two daughters, and is one hell of good welder. He can strike a bead from bottom to top, work that rod dancing his elbow left to right, fuse metal together with molten steel stronger than the original. You name it: TIG, MIG, Stick—the man's an artist. When he's not building gates or trailers, Joe looks after his four year old daughter, Vanessa, who, by the way, has him wrapped around her little finger. Vanessa recently lost her older brother in a car crash. So Joe spent 20 years as a law man protecting people and clearing the bad stuff out of the way, but he couldn't save his own son.

A few years back Joe killed a man in the course of duty. He did everything he was taught to do—the guy was seriously bad news and Joe took care of it. It was him or Joe in that moment, and probably a lot of other innocent people. But when it was all over neither the public nor his peers really understood Joe, nor backed him up. Joe says it's taking him years to undo the conditioning and sort through his feelings about all this. Another time, Joe told me, he was in the parking lot of the Blue Spruce down on Highway 84. Some lowlife had just stabbed him but Joe got the jump on him and held him at gun point in the gravel. This guy was total scum too; no one would have given a shit if they buried him before dawn. The man on the ground looked up at Joe with tears in his eyes and something shifted in Joe. He holstered his weapon and cuffed the guy. "Something changed for me that day," said Joe, "letting him live was a good thing."

Joe and I joke a little rough to get through the hard times. When

126

some selfish asshole—an arrogant outsider being a common
target—is making life difficult for the people around us Joe says,
"Let's just take him up to cottonwood tree and hang him up-
side-down for the coyotes. But my favorite is thirty days in the
electric chair. It's just a difference in upbringing I guess.

Some days when we're working together and the wind's blowing
hard Joe says, "I hate the wind. It was blowing hard that day
too, the day I killed that man." At those moments what I really
want to say is that I'm sorry about his boy, but we're not going
there yet. A man needs time to do that work in his own way. And
what's more, if anybody thinks being a law man is just heartless
machismo, then they can stand in a puddle of water and grab the
electrodes while I walk over here and turn on the welder. That's
the way Joe and I talk to one another. It's an economy of bravado
covering hurt. But for all our posturing, if a real situation came
down I know that Joe wouldn't let me do anything stupid; he
wouldn't let me hurt myself or anyone else. He'd talk to me
about honesty and responsibility and making choices, and when
the storm had passed we'd joke about the next likely candidate
for the cottonwood tree.

Orange Hills, Holy Water

A ripple of birds turn
at my window and I wonder
at the message they bring. Tomorrow
my own heart flies

to the orange hills of Ojo Caliente.
How we laid in that bed,
day and night dancing
around us, coyotes

coming in, *orejas* to the wind,
el sonido de la 'céquia.
Some smoke has disappeared;
I swear, there was a fire here.

I will be your anthropologist. Look,
here is where we washed the babies;
here men named the stars; here
is the stain of blood that follows us,

the decision to be on our own.
Put your hand in the shimmering spring;
this is the holy water that calls us.
You and I are none other than this.

Proof of Address

This is how it worked: we'd start off with a morning A.A. meeting in Taos, drive to the hot springs at Ojo Caliente for a soak, then go over the pass for an enchilada dinner in El Rito. A perfect winter day. This was before the fire at Ojo so the pools were segregated and enclosed. The men's pool, now called the Iron Pool, was dark, low-ceilinged and dimly lit with candles. The hotter spots were near the large rusty formation that had built up, and is still being built up, with sediment over which the warm subterranean waters flow. It was cave-like with whispered voices and dripping water echoing in the semi-darkness. It was a womb. Perhaps the best offering was the free Milagro Wrap. Following your soak in warm mineral waters you were given the opportunity to lay on a table in a quite and ancient adobe room and be gently wrapped in layers of muslin and covered with a wool blanket by attendants, soft spoken Hispanos who lived in the valley. They would check on you from time to time, offer to wipe the sweat from your eyes and help you off the table when fully cooked. After all that camaraderie, relaxing waters, loving touch, and a sunset drive in brisk mountain air we were indeed ready for some serious red chile and sopapillas at Farolito's.

Years later, and after the ownership of Ojo Caliente Mineral Springs had changed hands, I began contracting to the springs as an IT Consultant. The new owners, a Louisiana family whose fortune gushes from the manufacture and sales of off-shore drilling equipment with contracts around the world, purchased the property "as is," and have put several million dollars into its restoration—a monumental task. Their youngest son, an avid recreationalist who traveled the world engaging in extreme sports, moved to New Mexico at 26 years of age and was installed as the executive manager of what is now advertised as a resort and spa. This gave the family more direct control over a business that was clearly out of their scope of experience and an opportunity for their son to come in off the surf board and learn about the practice of business—also a monumental task.

The new executive manager, having no experience in spiritual practice nor in healing communities, has put his energy into refurbishing the physical infrastructure and building new lodging units that provide a substantial increase in revenue. Perhaps more high-minded and evolved endeavors are to follow, but certainly these newcomers have brought the hot springs to the next level in terms of sanitation and technology while focusing on its financial success by targeting the "spa crowd." A few years ago I was brought on board as operations manager and took a full time job, a position that I soon aborted. I left exhausted and bewildered like many before and after me who have assisted the family as they assert their corporate presence in New Mexico. I returned to the San Luis Valley about the time they moved the Milagro Wrap to the back room of a less charming building and started charging money for that ancient amenity. But first, this brief but all consuming job required that I move down from Del Norte, Colorado to the Ojo Caliente area. I chose La Madera, eight miles north of the springs.

La Madera [lumber], was the scene of a logging and lumber boom that brought short-lived economic development to northern New Mexico and delivered building materials to large western cities in the mid to later 1900s. Just as the rails (pulled up when no longer needed) took the forest to Albuquerque and Denver, so, too, did the hope of establishing a better future for the children of Vallecitos and La Madera vanish when there was no more gain for outsiders. Evidence of better years can be seen in some of the remaining structures, one of which is the old Mercantile now the residence of James Mustoe, a landscaper and artist living on a precarious edge of the grid just below the highway. The only activity in town with any regularity is Mass at 4:30 PM on Saturdays—the hand-rung bell clanging fifteen minutes early to give the few local devotees time to wash up and walk over to the chapel. Other than that, you might catch Jimmy or Connie Ortega at the Apache Drum store, the only retail business in town, and one that doesn't abide by any set hours and is therefore more in tune with the ebb and flow of daily life in the valley.

Jimmy Ortega's great grand father was an Apache Genízaro who worked for the Lucero family at Ojo Caliente. His son, Jimmy's grandfather, was adopted as a boy by the Ortega family, another prominent Hispanic family in the area. Prominence in Norteño some times does, and some times does not, have any thing to do with financial wealth, just as true machismo has more to do with graciousness, pride and looking after those less fortunate than it does with posturing or bravado. Jimmy Ortega has true machismo. His wife Connie began working at the springs many years ago tucking people into Milagro Wraps then worked her way into running the front desk and finally into a position as comptroller. She has trained hundreds of young women and men, teaching them the skills and giving them the confidence they needed to go beyond the valley and establish themselves elsewhere in the world.

I rented a hundred year old two-room adobe house in downtown La Madera, which is to say, I lived two houses behind Apache

Drum and a hundred yards from most people in the village. I wrote several poems from The Weight of Dusk that summer while thunderstorms pelted the rusting iron roof and plum trees grew like weeds. Once I had to take a 60 mile detour to work when heavy rains coming off Comanche Ridge washed out the road. I don't know if the best love-making is before, during or after a storm, but I recommend all three.

When I first moved to the area I went down to Española to get a driver's license. I had been warned about the Española MVD and took the entire day off. In the course of the day I was number 8, number 98 and number 163, making trips to the County Assessor and other official sites, including two trips back to La Madera. It was beyond Homeland Security. It was the dysfunctional and well entrenched left over system whereby the Spanish brought civilization to the natives and the U.S. government picked up the whip and laid down yet another twelve layers of red tape on top of that. It was like confession with skin offerings. Take a novel and some heroin.

When I was number 98 the clerk behind bullet-proof glass asked for my physical address. "My what?" I began describing La Madera, a village not known by its addresses but whether a house is on either the east side or the west side of the highway. "My house," I explained, "is on the west side near the church." She was not amused, nor were the other customers who waited with their babies, their lunches and their non-English speaking grandmothers while seeking numbness in the looming presence of three television sets hanging from the walls. Grappling with my homicidal feelings but somewhat controlled for the moment I went back to La Madera a second time and to the Post Office. There, Diolynda Peña, the exceptionally beautiful postmistress who makes all the men nervous and the women wag their tongues, puzzled with me over this new issue of assigning an address to my house. We went outside and were standing in the middle of the intersection of State Highways 111 and 519, a crossroad in which you could stand for a half hour without needing to move to the side. While trying to come up with a name for the dirt lane to my house Jimmy Ortega showed up in his telephone truck while out fixing lines downed by thunder storms and promising DSL (any month now).

Jimmy joined us at the crossroads in front of his store and in a moment of regal authority (he was, after all, head of the Water Association) declared that the lane to my house should be called County Road 1694, and further more that my house should be #2. It was done. Diolinda wrote it on a piece of paper and I went back to the MVD feeling a bit shaky about the whole thing and hoping they wouldn't check it against some hidden records once held by the King of Spain. I was the last person to be let in as it was the end of the day. By the time the light flashed 163 there were just two of us at the windows. When asked for my address I feigned assurance and said, "#2, County Road 1694." She promptly stamped a piece of paper without looking up and directed me to the camera. It took me a moment to regain myself.

I had this floating sensation as if I had just left purgatory and entered a world with less gravity and sweetly tweeting birds. In fact, the guy at the other window began singing a show tune from the Sound of Music with much volume and gusto. What a character! All the employees, who earlier in the day had looked like gargoyles guarding the Department of Mind Control, came out of back offices to listen and then they applauded.

After the Rain

Wild plum branches
  like dogs
    lie in piles, wet

greenness twisting
  for light.
    Shovels strike

rock, the men
  return, grunting
    toward pipe.

At night
  the giant cottonwood
    is quiet. At night

window music
  pours
    over muddy fields.

On the other side,
  someone
    calling his dog.

Steal This Poem

The resort hotel purchased a Buddha,
cast cement, painted black,
Indonesian style, hands: one up
and one down, mudras above and below,
and placed him in a nicho
along the sacred walk between
massage rooms and mineral pool.
Reposed and recessed
into faux adobe wall he waits;
he does not wait, his eyes
are both open and closed.

In front of his crossed legs
with foot cradled in crook of knee,
a dried flower stalk of nothing famous
lay south to north, red yarn
tied at its base (a pilgrim's gift)
and in his receptive left palm
a crystal cluster had been fixed.

"Good idea," an employee remarked,
noting the permanence of quartz
glued with Epoxy against theft,
the hotel securing its assets,
supporting that popular belief
that what one gets one must steal.
Then, steal this crystal!

Steal these offerings, chip away

at my feet, toes at a time;
knock off these shoulders, this head;
cart away whatever is between us.

Nothing real can be removed,
my eyes open only to that
which we are.

It Appears I Leave

Before fish walked the rock broke,
hot water charged with earth soul
shouted back to the sun, settled
as regenerating pools, singing streams.

I was born that morning, crack
of shell, plate unhinged, a song
already placed; the Cerro Colorado
announcing love throughout the sky.

I stood on the shores of rock and thought,
drank winds small from lizards, large
from blue stars, made waves of my own,
witnessed as each tribe came and went.

Arrived, they named rivers and boundaries;
called it green, called it hot.
They called it theirs—all this claiming, this show
of nudging one another off the branch.

In my many hands I've washed the babies
in steaming pools, made myself into mud things,
strung hope and wire, spoke with satellites.
Tomorrow I will cross the sky in great arcs.

Yesterday I entered the village as a tinker,
my satchel humming with colors and thanks.
As a traveller I appear—come, then go—
as the heart of Ojo, I remain.

Evening in Carson

In a stir of fireflies
    the earth makes us,
        holds us for a moment.

The wind lifts
    and whirrs. Leaves
        and winged seeds

fly up, a funnel of wrappers,
    some bone dust in the air.
        In a pale desert sky

contrails crisscross
    then disappear.
        I try to remember

everyone I meet
    but full communion waits.
        In the meantime this campfire

and your hand holding mine
    under the cool red shelf
        of sunset.

Brother André
from *Monastery of Christ in the Desert*

You will bend to brush
the ashes from my shoe,
hang my hat and coat, seat me
at your table;
your simple bowl
and morning song sure
as the mountain above you.

When you close the book,
lay it on the table the same
as every other evening,
that gesture flies
like a song from your bell,
a soft red bird
beneath my usual clatter.

When I arrive, I will have forgotten.

You'll show me my place again,
patiently, as if it were the first.
We'll sit at the long table,
two men nodding in silence,
remembering
that we have the same father.

La Piedra Lumina

High cold quilt of cloud,
murmur of juniper birds,
the story of morning rising
from luminous stone, bones
painted, scattered, red
drapes parted in columns.

The shadow masking one hill
reveals another behind it.
I look beyond the burnished sky—
not for a way out—
but to call the rest of me here.
Canyon, mesa, mountain;
canyon, cholla, lavender smoke.

I call across water
and where water used to be;
I see signs everywhere:
your clay shell crumbling,
destined wings unfolding, wild dogs
doing what they've always done.

We devour the world to save ourselves,
to hold our moment in time.
I'm more at home with the wind,
a pilgrim here.
I do not know the size of this earth
though I measure it step by step,
bowing, throwing myself forward,

rising up to praise again.

One thing for sure—
you have a place here
at the feet of Cerro Perdernal.
I left the sky just as I found it;
I moved the wood
a little closer to the door.

Echo Amphitheatre

Strong bluffs bare ancient shoulders
up Abiquiu way, orange scouts
above the rivier, *las viejas*
guarding the entry.

Carved by wind song and water's
flaming way, a towering shell
opens to the desert,
breathing stone, damp vagina.

Here in the echo chamber
of earth's pink heart a sent song returns.
The wise traveller listens first,
any rock or twig the messenger.

I went there with a flute
to hear myself reflected.
I was wrong. Not myself
in this time, not this self.

So I drafted a song and sent it on,
not knowing if you'd find it
up ahead, or if you're the one
who left it here for me.

Coming Out for Dinner

At the top of Trujillo Hill
I follow a two-track through white grasses,
their curly awns catching last light like
celebrants clutching candles,
a tide of mourners chanting,
"Holy is the earth."
The abrupt rock faces of Chinle Red
and Entrada Yellow pale and blur
in that final shadow as we turn,
now, away from the sun.

The Rio Chama flows
through massive cliffs, twists
around fallen boulders, divides and spreads
into a valley of cottonwoods,
spring buds so tight and full
I can hear their intention, intention
joining with the song of frogs—
first performance of the season.

Down river warm interior lights
of Abiquiu Inn play up
as a band of turquoise sky recedes
behind the silhouette of Sierra Negra.
I could be a stagecoach driver
taking wonder-filled but bemused travellers
back to the United States.
But tonight I'm a freed captive,

red dust on my boots, bullets
jangling with change in my pocket,
a hankering for colonial ways:
coffee from Peru; silver on cloth;
classical guitar from Seville;
that polite bilingual waiter.

Each room of the Inn is hung with art:
clouds and mesas applied
with broad knifes; a pair of almond eyes
tugging us back to the bedroom,
watermelons and chapels in pointillism,
landscape paintings that have little
to do with the land.
I steal a last look toward Polvadera
and hear spurs clinking
on the portal, an artist
trading for kerosene and cornmeal.

On my way home I circle the lake,
dark fingers of land reaching
across starlit water
thinning to extinction, dying
like memories without touching.
There are no mileage signs
to my town, just two dead taverns
and forgotten fruit trees that push
through the floorboards of a village
that drives two hours to find work.
In the morning when again we turn
toward the light,
I'll begin a new painting.

Springtime Comes to Ritos de los Encinos

Mud—wind—peep of green—graduation.
Underground, prairie dogs teach vigilance,
cattle dance loose on the garden,
a true *vecino* welcomes the newcomer
and a mile high *terremote* spins red
with the dust of departed souls.
I go to Cuba for a wheel barrow,

handful of bolts, biscuits and gravy,
a side of red, some local talk;
like a Robin my ear to the ground.
In San Yisidro a woman
with full dark hair dangles her feet
over a scaffold, slings wet orange earth

on a house, smoothes the sun
into an east-facing wall—
a spider building with elements of herself.
I pass slowly, a movie maker
panning for stories, sifting gold,
learning to finally see with these eyes.

It's no longer enough
to take off another skin. One day
I'll begin every sentence with love.
One day I won't have to
choose again. Everything I made up
about you, happily, was wrong.

Christ!

The only way to get there was to leave Taos at 2:30 am on a winter morning which would put me at Ghost Ranch when it was still dark and well below freezing, in fact usually between 10 and 20 degrees. Otherwise the 13 mile dirt road to Monastery of Christ in the Desert was ten inches of soupy mud ruts that would swallow my car or throw it off the cliff. In the early hours of the morning, before the road began to thaw, I could keep the old Pontiac on top of the frozen ruts all the way up to the monastery and let myself in to the Guest House while it was still dark. Brother André would have unlocked my room and all I needed to do was light the little stove and settle in with books and writing paper.

The cell was about eight feet square with one door, one window, a small wood stove, two concrete boncos on opposite walls, and a wooden table between them with a kerosene lantern and a bible. The only adornment, a cross on the wall, was often made of palm leaves tied in a knot to form the dissecting planes of heaven and earth, the union of man and god, symbol of death and resurrection. One day Brother André and I took a walk up river past the Hermit's Cabin, and into the forest. At one point he made a pass at me, which I declined. We walked on continuing our visit along the Ponderosa-needled path next to the Rio Chama, then returned to the community. The next day he invited me into the quiet of his office and apologized for what he called his "brokenness," asking for my forgiveness. Having hit the road at thirteen, been in and out jails and spent time on the farm, I've been approached for a lot things in a lot of different ways. I didn't have a problem with his request and knew how to politely say "no thanks." What I was having angst about at the moment were the Four Pillars of the Church and why it insisted on trying to draw relevance from stories that pre-dated Jesus and represented the unhealed, unconscious state of humanity.

Though I'm not Catholic I was exposed to "The Church" when my mother remarried. I even did a year in boarding school run by Augustinians. And now my quest to find the mystic in all forms of devotion had run me up against the "brokenness" of the Catholic Church. The divine in man takes a lot of nasty twists and turns when it's run through the filter of fear. The Crusades of Europe and the terror propaganda following 911 being two horrid examples. So, there was the age-old question: How can a grossly fallible system hold a claim on truth and deliver the sacrament to the public? Intellectually I knew the answer, but I needed to heal this wound down deep, through lifetimes.

The custom of this Abbey, run by Benedictines, is to chant eight time a day, beginning with Vigils at 4:am. So the next morning I bundled up, braced myself for the cold, and crunched down the dark road to the Chapel to participate in this eight hundred year old ritual while the secular world slept. I got there early and sat by myself in one of the guest pews. One thing I appreciate about the Abbey is its lack of gilding. The altar is a square platform in the center of the room that gets covered with a plain cloth and is devoid of paraphernalia or icons. The rest of the Chapel is similarly simple. In this sanctuary of silence and in the absence of distraction all I could think of at that moment was the brutality and arrogance of the works we were about to chant—calling upon God to smite our enemies in the name of righteousness, and worse. I felt sick.

With only few exceptions the Psalms of the Old Testament which make up the bulk of the chants, are some of the most violent writings in western literature. It felt then that 2,000 years of gross misunderstanding and blatant misuse of the mystic teachings were pressing down upon me. And at that moment I looked up and took notice of the only other fixture in the Chapel, a nearly life-sized statue of Jesus elevated in the eastern wing. "Why?" I complained out loud.

"That's why I'm here," he answered in the silent authority of my heart," to bring the new law: Have love one for another even as I have love for you."

The conflict was unbearable: the continuous cycle of unconscious harming of ourselves and therefore of one another, followed by remorse and penance, followed by supplication, followed by more unconscious violence. "I hate you, I'm bad, I'm sorry, I hate you...."

And there was Christ shining through it all, bringing the new law without condemnation, without fail. I gave up fighting, trying to understand, trying to change the entire world, and began crying so hard I fell on the woven grass mat on the floor in front of me.

I sobbed uncontrollably, aware only later that André and the other brothers had entered, picked up their books and begun chanting as they have always done. No one bothered me or tried to take away my tears as my wailing echoed in the dimly lit chapel and into the dark desert. They simply held that sacred space as I'm sure they have done for many a seeker before me. If for a brief time I had considered joining The Church it was clear now that it was not my path. After my last experience at

the Abbey at Christ in the Desert I realized that membership in
The Church would be going backward for me, reliving a lifetime
already lived. Without the burden of religion I was now free to
share the teachings with other wanderers on the desert who need
only know where they can find the water, and that they are loved
without merit and beyond measure.

Sopapilla Delivery
for Amie D. Martinez, Postmaster, Youngsville, N. Mex.

Thunder rumbled behind the mesas
so when Amie knocked I thought
it was the tall walking rain
and went on working
upstairs in the old farmhouse

while darkness settled slowly,
withdrawing shapes at the edge.
That's not always how it is. You remember
friends abruptly falling off the path
without a shout, without a moan;

no twilight to prepare us,
no raven at the window. Last month
three boys met head-on on the highway
between this town and the next.
Everyone warned the woman,

but you can't stop a mother
from standing flat-footed
before the cart of death, peering
with a flashlight into the wrecks.
You can't pull her away

until she's sure that her boys
are far from those mangled bodies,
are, somehow, not those bodies at all.
Later Amie called and said,

"We would have honked

but the horn on the truck is broken,
do you want some fresh *sopapillas?*"
Tonight her babies are safe at home,
bigger ones tending smaller ones, stacks
of warm *sopas* on the table, enough

for her children and her neighbors,
for everyone in town and the next town over.
Enough for that other mother
and for those boys out on the highway
trying to get home before they get cold.

Onion River

The Onion River runs across the night
side by side with restless horses,
their painted riders; runs
through herds of sleeping sheep
unseen by hostile tribes, runs
behind the towns built by captives
that will one day fly like burnt paper.

The Onion River floats like a moth;
nothing can touch her. Only you and I
can feel her, a flower that opens
after dark, a loose ribbon.
The Genízaros of Canjilon
cut wood for the winter.
Back and forth they make the crossing;
rocky ford, squeaky springs,
feathers on the dash,
a tiger in hidding.

The Onion River has no eyes,
no tomorrows; no one knows for sure
where she begins.
Sometimes she's nothing but stars,
sometimes Venus is bright enough
to read your own hand. You can
hear her whisper, hear her moan;
you can hunt beyond the border
for miles and miles and miles.

The sputter of a round fire
against yellow rock is reason enough
to linger inside; the steam rising
in dark marshes is the Onion River
coming up for air. We kissed
on the tongue of night, then
I watched as you flew west.

A dance hall for trout,
a mirror for mountain lion,
the Onion River's a sigh
flat out for the moon.
In the high country we live
dusk to dusk, every living being
eventually to the watering hole;
every eventuality
falling in love again.

Bullets in Firewood

"Throw your shoes in after the match," he said. We were discussing arson. I was sharing my consternation about the abandoned single-wide on the property west of me. It had long since been left for the prevailing, and often gale-force, winds that rip down off the San Pedro Mountains and out across the Piedra Lumbre. From time to time jagged pieces of metal siding and large yellow clumps of asbestos insulation would sail over the fence and up against my door. What was left of the mobile home leaned into the red dirt like a cripple with the crutches kicked out from under it, and I could see trucks on the other side rolling down Highway 96 through the skewed frame of what was once the living room. Kitchen cabinet doors banged and occasionally the entire structure groaned and settled perking the ears of prairie dogs who lived under it. "Just toss your shoes in to remove any evidence and walk away," Abel said, "by the time the Volunteer Fire Department gets here there won't be anything left."

Abel was once again giving me good practical advice about living in the Youngsville-Coyote area. I'd stopped by to borrow a digging bar for setting a fence post and he was taking an afternoon break from a plastering job and looking after his two-year old son, Santos. We sat at the kitchen table talking while Santos toddled, wide-eyed with arms up giving the world his innocent blessing. His older brother A.J. hovered over him mimicking his tiny steps, ready to provide redirection. Once in a while Santos would have an altercation with a table leg or his face would find the floor. In this case Abel would beckon him to his chair and lift him onto his lap gently brushing the pain from his scrunched up

154

face but without any of the doting that women do, just a non-assuming presence—"food from men's bodies," that's what Robert Bly calls it.

Abel is stout and strong and his demeanor calm. It takes a lot to rattle him. He holds the energy in a room like a pin driven with a sledge three feet into the ground. He'd just gotten a haircut and the little bit on top that he could comb was slicked back. He was wearing a new black T-shirt that day. We talked cars, drugs, drinking and jail, but there was never any boasting, just how it used it be: racing on the main drag in Cuba, N. Mex., outwitting the cops by turning his lights out and laying low on a forest service road for three hours. Abel turned the corner earlier than a lot of his friends. He doesn't like jail, doesn't like wrecking cars, doesn't see any gain in repeating the pattern. This sets him apart from some of his people, from what he calls "*mi raza*." If Abel betters himself some of his old friends are suspicious, jealous. If not, then he does little for his own family, and his pride. He's an example for his community and it cost him. Abel walks that fine edge and the things he sees and wants to change for his children and his nieces and nephews are big, big like the mesa above his town that runs east to west as far as you can see, inescapably part of his landscape. So much beauty; so much pain.

Beauty and pain are the apple and knife of the world, and in Norteño we shine the one and sharpen the other with a passion Like matter and anti-matter the two propel us through our lives. The Piedra Lumbre Basin is a theatre of passion with its history of boundaries that shifted seasonally as we battled over this jewel of the earth. Over the last 600 years, and probably longer, people have sought beauty and sustenance here despite tremendous hardship. Prehistoric farmers, hunting tribes, homesteading

Europeans, everyone that has entered this country has been driven back or captured in one way or another. Groups taking turns raiding the villages and camps of others has been commonplace, human beings bought, sold and slaughtered. This place has always been the rough edge of the world where cultures clash. And like tumbleweeds in autumn, our hold on the land eventually became tenuous, the winds of change ripping out roots and sending us on our way, another non-native temporarily taking its place. But in this modern period of apparent peace the forces of subjugation are at work more than ever. As I sat talking with Abel I looked into the addition he had built onto his home and there were the shackles of the new system of bondage: a wide screen TV and a remote.

If Abel doesn't give his family these "conveniences" he's not a good provider; he's a traitor somehow, a crazy man. His children need this digital connection to society so they can live in the world. But the cost is brutal. From it they learn fear, learn to be obedient consumers, to be the commodity itself. It's one thing to see a raiding party of Apaches coming over the ridge or the Spanish militia driving up the valley with horses and metal, but like smallpox traveling silently in the body of one seafaring conquistador the new mode of slavery has already been quietly established. Dictates no longer come from The Crown or The Papacy in Europe but from an amorphous American convention called the Corporatocracy. How, my brother Abel, shall we fight these marauders?

Abel would say I take myself too seriously. Perhaps. Perhaps he knows much more than I when it comes to fighting these cunning new adversaries. I watch him at his annual family reunion up in the mountains standing over a homemade propane stove stirring pounds of *pollo, steak, cebolla and chiles*, cooking for his family. Sometimes he feigns frustration at requests from family, just enough to show he's not taking orders from the women, then, he takes orders from his wife, his mother, his grandmother, serving his people *como un Hermano*, a true leader-servant. But he doesn't put up with immature bull shit. When one of the guys gets out of line all he needs to do is frown and shake his head. He's kicked enough ass in the past that people know he can take care of business. With that established, he goes about his business stashing money for his daughter's graduation and teaching his sons and nephews how to work with the men without whining. As a peacekeeper, Abel's way of teaching is by not engaging in that old crap that hurts the community, his people, my people.

On another afternoon Abel told me how some cousins were stealing firewood from him when he lived in a family *placita* down in Arroyo de Agua. No one admitted to the theft but, as always, he knew who was doing it. "I cured them of that," he said. Abel went out to the woodpile with a cordless drill and a box of bullets, drilled holes in pieces of *leña* and inserted live ammo. He made sure his Aunt was watching and when she came out of her house alarmed and squawking he told her that he was tired of having people steal from him and so he was putting bullets in the firewood. Word spread like a prairie dog infestation. His little trick got the point across—no more stolen firewood. Later he said, "I didn't really put the bullets in there; all I had to do was act like it." I'm still not sure if he actually put the bullets in the wood or not but the idea of dealing with thieves in that way is often appealing to me. In fact, I think I'll notify my bank that if they send another scary advertisement for theft protection or life insurance or up my interest rate without recourse I'm going to put bullets in my payment envelopes.

Mesa Prieta
for Laurie and Jared

At dusk she pulls her children close,
one eye cocked on a quarrel
of coyotes, a rattler missing a mouse,
your straw house curled at her feet.
    Storms and kites both rise and fall,
    but she stays through the night.

At dawn she invites the light:
high ochre walls, white drapes,
juniper staircases flowing down,
the living earth thrusting up;
wind, the beginning of birds.
    Your home is this good fortune
    where ravens dive and turn.

Shadows make their way over the *llano*,
slip into crimson canyons, swim
to the top, die into the open-armed sky.
Mesa Prieta, legend and flesh,
waits with a song at your window.
    You brought your lover to this high desert.
    Now, abandon all promises.

Toward La Vida

Curtains of desert rain shape-shift through the Bistahi Badlands,
tangles of white wires arc wildly, sting the earth in long kisses.
The unending thunder wanders north.

Raven wings wink in sudden sun. Flash flood! I'm staggering
across the top of a world, woozy from a day I can't name. If I've
forgotten something important—all the better—importance was
such a distraction.

Horses move at an easy pace along the ridge. If you follow them
all day this land will scatter your bones, and any ideas of the
world will be replaced with water.
A half a day ago some sheep.

On the opposite side of the Chaco River endless shelves of pale
green bleed red through the fresh bone of this earth, the marrow
exposed, the horses making their way, higher. Turn in every
direction; who's life do you see here?

Your own tracks going back on this muddy road; cool rivulets
pulling fine sand from under harder stones; a piece of petrified
wood; a new lavender flower lifting its head, looking around.

The water goes down. The horses move up. The wind creates the
world from nothing: small birds, fragrances, horizons. Tell me,
who lives here?

Coming from Aneth

> "Just like the devil" was the term applied
> to the business practice of the community's
> first Anglo trader. So Aneth was given
> the same name in Diné.

We push away
from our overflowing tables,
as we push our way
through blaring households
overflowing into storage units,
into the 'away place',
into arroyos where we park cars
like broken pottery pushed
from convenient cliffs.

We push the world
out of our way
in search of a world
who's teeth won't chatter;
in search of the monolith,
the movie star state,
a cleaner history,
a town without ghosts.

In some way
that is related to blood,
but not of it,
I am pushing out from myself,
free grazing with horses

on the hillside, tracking
invisible buffalo, stumbling
over casinos and
sandwich shop rubble.

I am going nowhere,
and now I finally understand
that Four Corners isn't about
the coincidence of state lines
but standing still in the sun
and letting all the winds
come at once.

Shiprock,
I am moving toward you
and always away from you,
and I am afraid
of becoming too much
like myself, too much
like the postcard
they have planned for you.
A whirling devil
has crossed the road
in front of us.

But in this desert country
I see how things wait
for their own season,
sleep on top of water,
push a little—then pull back.
And whatever is here
or not here is spun

by invisible winds, currents
that carve pink and white hearts
from the bottom of the ocean,
that find red fish folded,
still smiling,
in the water pockets.

Gathering at Kin Kletso

The wind in Chaco Canyon: stern.
Coyote didn't show
but the rocks kept kissing,
presenting enormous faces.
Tell me about lizard, you said,
about Kokopelli. Take me
out on the mesa and show me
how we stood and waved
back at the stars.

I was a potter building songs.
That was you at the wall
etching the rain, those powdery grains
falling from an ocean bed—
the fine edge of your flint blade.
You dreamed going home.

At dawn you stood on the edge of a cliff
and threw a basket of cornmeal
into the sky. Whatever was said was sent.

That night a woman
stumbled into our camp,
reported descending several kivas.
In one, she said,
I felt dizzy, stunned; my guides told me
it was a satellite dish left turned on.
Later we chanted the moon,
slipped into rock.

Navajoland, West of Nageezi

Everything is made of white,
almost invisible, ripples.
That lizard, that rock, those car parts.
The days here are poured west
through distant storms,
firewalls, violet ice, silhouette,
silence. Night
is a word that means remember.

Everything located here loses it's name.
Nothing stays the same.
Even the wind sleeps dreaming
new faces over the land.
I could remain a stranger,
but I sense a self everywhere:
at the base of a layered wash
curving pink;
in the wake of a wing;
a voice from the ground.

Walking at dusk a Cliffrose
stopped me on the path to talk,
suggested I wear pale yellow in my speech,
sandstone shoes.
I have believed too much.
I have believed too many things.
I am leaving myself
for the wind.

Silence, but That Was Just a Word

In Perfect Time

Flirting back and forth in the brilliant sun,
taking turns at the lilac, the hanging chile,
then the antique rose, the hummingbird
sought blooms already delivered.

Go south, I said, unnecessarily.
It was September at eight thousand feet
and though the light was shrinking,
shot through with invisible fissures

by a dimension ready to replace it,
the last hollyhock continued to hold
the blue prayer shawl of sky pinned to the horizon—
and the earth, because it belongs

to that family whose nature it is to give
and to renew, turned in perfect time
with the comings and goings of hummingbirds,
the distribution of light, the fallen petal of summer.

In the Morning, a Leaf

It had come with an armload
of firewood last night and now
sat silently on the painted
plywood floor of the cabin,
December brown, lifeless
most folks would say.

As I lit a fire in the bath
then roughed up embers
in the big cast iron and moved
my bright red cup to the table,
I found myself
stepping around it—the leaf.

I don't get many visitors out here
I started to say, then
looking up I felt everything
I ever touched touch me back.
And all that I can name:

turquoise window frame, blue light
singing in snow shadow,
feathers fadding on the dash,
wrinkle of open sky
around each earthly thing

spoke, so to speak,
and I, a lucky leaf,
having entered this house, marveled

before tall straw broom, gurgling kettle,
a man extending
beyond the roots of his previous self.

Brilliant

Dark fog turned to snow storms
across Christmas (that tenuous spark
hovering in the cold glow of retail)
but as promised, the light returned.

Six days past solstice the sky
has opened, an eye stretching wide
to see itself, embrace
this babe of a world.
Puffy birds, sun-colored stalks,
jack rabbit, rancher,
travellers in skins, the frozen road—
all lifting in unison.

Today Jorge and his wife from Alcalde
make the drive to Nido del Cielo
to purchase my other woodstove.
The wind cuts, she says,
but her lack of attack tells me
she's at peace with it.

I mention a back injury
as we close the tailgate. She says,
four doctors wanted to operate
with knives. She doesn't
pray to their god, either.

Here, in this place some call
the edge, but others feel

172

to be the center, snow
has drifted in unsuspected ways
to create a fresh and forgiven world—
brilliant, touchable, seen.

Adrift, Essentially

Fluffy cottonwood seeds catch
in the wispy arms of nodding grass,
release, hesitate, drift
on solar winds rising
from a warm flagstone path.

Twirling slowly between twigs,
people, telephone poles,
they have no need
for reincarnation, systems
of moral selection, the soul.

Today

A white feather fell
as I stood at the pond; reflections
of trees fully dressed and naked,
frog eyes, insect ripple,
pink going to white across blue.

Tiny feather, this
eyelash descending soft
as an exhale, I could have caught it
on a single finger. I could have.

But everywhere it rested it rested
in my heart. Today,
I said, I will choose again.

Bluebirds
for Ann McDaniel

Mountain Bluebirds descend the *cerro*
in underhanded swoops, tree to tree,
cholla to post, squint-eyed
they dive into the wind.
In mid-flight: blades on edge,
when hovering to land: flashes
of deep azure blue.

This life is everything I dream:
early morning fire in the stove;
coyboying on the *llano,*
hello's, goodbye's; reasons to go
down into the valley;
the local neighborhood
with clusters of light further out;
always some moments of hell
from horizon to horizon—
the bluebirds
stitching their way across the field.

What I dream seems to be
my own, then, she takes me
to the red place, to the white place.
She sees calico; I see galaxies,
every pebble formidable.
Ducks sit the river posting up and down.
Unseen waves pass through them.

Some days I sweep cobwebs
from the ceiling, some days
I stop, study them in awe.
It takes eight minutes
for what we call daylight to arrive
from the sun. I know stars
billions of light years away.
Some of them flash blue, too.

Standing Beside the House

I'm halfway there I tell myself
with no clue of what that means.
Quick to assign meaning, this mind
a meaning making machine.

When it gnaws at the moment
I toss it words; when it sleeps
I tiptoe between breaths.

Last night I crunched through snow
to stand beside the house, away
from the manufactured earth.

Above me the deep and present,
below me the same. Silence,
but that was just a word. I,
but no I was there.